Q&A WITH A PK

Growing up as a Preacher's Kid

By

Jonathan D. Weinberg

The contents of this work, including, but not limited to, the accuracy of events, people, and places depicted; opinions expressed; permission to use previously published materials included; and any advice given or actions advocated are solely the responsibility of the author, who assumes all liability for said work and indemnifies the publisher against any claims stemming from publication of the work.

Dorrance Publishing Co
585 Alpha Drive
Pittsburgh, PA 15238
Visit our website at *www.bookstore.dorrancepublishing.com*

ISBN: 978-1-6491-3130-0
EISBN: 978-1-6491-3637-4

For Zack, Dani and Joey

Table of Contents

Introduction

31E.

To the average person, it's just a random number and letter. To a seasoned business traveler, the number will jump off the page; horror, dread, dismay. 31E means a middle seat, and not just any middle seat, a middle seat in the back of the airplane.

Over the past six months, I have been on the road traveling from state-to-state to secure governmental regulatory approvals for the purchase of the company I work for. The travel is getting old, the airport food older, and as I sit in my tiny seat, my mind is filled with a lot of uncertainty. Having been a part of a company which had, in the past, acquired twenty five companies, I know the drill when it comes to corporate acquisitions and what that portends for the acquired company's executives. The polite term is "synergy," its real name is "termination" or "firing." I know what lies ahead of me. Now, the shoe is on the other foot, we are the ones who have been acquired, I know where the synergies are going to come from, and soon I will be unemployed.

My fellow seatmates settle in, one with his elbow firmly planted in my stomach, the others knee very uncomfortably resting on my leg; one with a hacking cough and one who takes out his McDonalds bag as we sit at the gate. The smell of his Big Mac permeates the air. The pilot comes over the PA to tell us,

"Folks, as soon as we are able to pull back we will get the air going, we know it's hot back there but it should only be another twenty minutes and we will be underway, appreciate your patience."

31E.

Try as I might not to let it happen, it does. I make eye contact with 31D and then it starts, every business traveler's second worst nightmare (next to the middle seat) the questions.

"Hey what line of work are you in? Where you from? Where you heading?"

On it goes, from work to travel to family, and then he gets to my parents, "what line of work where they in?"

"My dad was a rabbi," I reply.

"Wow, very cool, what was that like, I mean, having your dad as a pastor, that must have been different. I mean, I knew a kid growing up and his dad was a minister and his dad was really an authoritarian with him, nice enough kid, but must have been rough with his dad being a minister and all…"

On it goes, or should I say, on he goes.

The conversation and questions are all typical. I have had them numerous times with numerous people.

"You must have had a strict upbringing?"

"Did you have study the Torah every day?"

"Did you wear those curls in your hair?"

"Does you dad ever laugh or make jokes?"

As soon as you mention that your dad was a "man of the cloth," the floodgates open; everyone it seems becomes curious about your life.

Upon landing and heading home, I find myself at my desk late that night, changing out my folders and papers in my bag for the next trip two days later. As I sit at my desk, I see the stack of manila folders on the corner. They have been occupying that spot for some time now. In the folders are some of my father's sermons I have collected over the years. From time to time, I will pick one up. I'd like to think that soon I will show them to my kids, so they might get a little glimpse of their Papa Joe. From time to time, my siblings and I have contemplated compiling the sermons and publishing them, but then life seems to get in the way – work, business trips, kids, carpools, soccer games. The folders stay neatly stacked on the corner of the desk.

Why do the sermons just sit here? Why am I not doing something with them? Why, at age 45, have I been starring at the pile for so many years?

The guy from 31D and his questions pop back into my brain. I was hot, tired, and annoyed during the flight; not in much of a mood to recount stories about growing up with a dad who was a rabbi. I stare at the pile. My mind was swirling. Not ready to go to bed, I picked up one the folders and began to read one entitled *One Day More*. It was a sermon about his experience having open heart surgery.

> *This Rosh Hashanah (the Jewish holiday that celebrates the Jewish New Year) impels us toward new beginnings, to revise the habits and pattern of the past, to stretch, to reach for a finer quality of life, a more noble pathway. We do not have forever, the clock ticks away. Each evening's sunset punctuates the reality of our mortality and cries out, 'do not squander the gift of a new day.'*
>
> *How many times does a Rabbi preach this? But tonight my sermon is not of words, it is the experience I have lived. Healthy, jogging, a good diet. Suddenly an infection came destroying a heart valve. Open heart surgery is no stranger to someone who has been a rabbi for 25 years and knows the intensive care unit of every hospital in the city, but when it's you, oh my what a difference.*
>
> *Leaving your home for the hospital, the door closing, the driveway and neighborhood receding all the while wondering what will be? Will I return? Wheeled down the long hallway to the Operating Room, to kiss Marcia, Rachel, Jonathan and Joshua good bye, embracing them as never before. Reassuring each other but also knowing there are no guarantees. Going to sleep, will I awake? Will there be morning?*
>
> *And then that moment, blurry lights, dull foggy voices, images and faces and then a distant chant becomes real, "You're alright Joe." "You're going to be fine Daddy." A smile, a gentle touch that has forever etched itself in my consciousness.*
>
> *Each day increased strength and then full and complete healing. Oh what a blessing to be alive, to feel well again, to rejoice with loved ones. To taste the beauty of each day's sunrise and give thanks for the fullness of life at each sunset. To be given one more day.*

At that moment, with my job, my future somewhat uncertain, I heard by father talking to me.

"Jono," (this was Dad's name for me, rarely "Jonathan" never "John.") "It's time to stop looking at the pile, stop putting off what you can today to another day, It is time to write, it is time to share. Find a pen, get a pad of paper and get busy."

This book is an attempt to share what it's like to be a PK – a preacher's kid. To provide answers to all of those questions I would get growing up, and some that I still get to this day. To be a PK was (and is) an immediate sense of curiosity. Lots of kids have dads who are lawyers, and doctors and businessmen, but a dad who is a rabbi; there are not many of them around. The questions have a lot to do with curiosity about a rabbi. Who is that person really? When they leave the synagogue what are they really like? Questions for the PK are, in many cases, questions for the rabbi and, for that matter, any member of the clergy, they just did not want to go asking the rabbi or minister himself or herself. The PK seemed like a safer person to approach with these types of inquiries.

In answering these questions, I hope to provide a window into the life of my father, Rabbi Joseph Weinberg, through some of his sermons and writings, as well as some of my writings and reflections about my dad. Through some of the unique stories of being a PK, I hope to provide you a slice of his life, some of his words and messages, and my life as a PK. Before I start answering the questions, some context should be provided.

Joseph Weinberg was born and raised in Chicago, Illinois. He attended Northwestern University as an undergraduate, and then enrolled at The Hebrew Union College in Cincinnati, Ohio. He was ordained as a rabbi in 1963. After serving a congregation in San Francisco for five years, he came to Washington, DC in 1968, where he served the Washington Hebrew Congregation. In 1986 Dad was elected as just the fifth Senior Rabbi of the congregation.

Washington Hebrew Congregation (WHC) is not your typical synagogue. It is big – really big. With approximately three thousand families, it is one of the country's largest. WHC is a reform congregation located in Northwest Washington, DC just over the DC/Maryland line. (Judaism has three major branches – orthodox, conservative, and reform. Reform Jews are the most liberal of the three, and take a more modern, less literal/observant view of the religion. It is not to say Reform Jews are not as religious, that is not the case, rather, we choose to practice in a different, less traditional manner.)

I grew up in Potomac, Maryland, one of the suburbs right outside Washington DC. Potomac has a huge Jewish population, probably one-third of the residents of Potomac are Jewish, and a large portion of that population are members of WHC. Dad often used the term, our "WHC family." He meant it as an endearing term. He felt close to all the members of the Temple. His calling was to serve and help each of them, and he did just that for 31 years at WHC. Growing up, my sister's room was next door to mine, my brother's room was next to hers, and our parents down the hall. However, our "WHC family" they were across the street, down the block, around the corner, at my elementary school, middle school, high school, on my soccer team, at the check-out line at the grocery store, and even in line at the local Roy Rodgers fast food restaurant on one of those days I decided to skip a few classes in high school. In Potomac, Maryland WHC family was everywhere.

I grew up the middle child. My sister, Rachel, is four years older, and my brother Josh is two years younger. Rachel and Josh were more than just my siblings growing up. Rachel and Josh were part of the small PK fraternity, mainly just the three of us. We did not know and were not friends with other kids whose parents where rabbis in the community. When dad was the junior rabbi, we were still very young. The Temple's then Senior Rabbi's kids were fully grown, off in college, and only one who was in high school. We did not spend a lot of time around them, so they never showed us the ropes. The junior rabbis who came to WHC when we got older all had infants or toddlers, fun to babysit once in a while, but there was no real PK bonding. It was really just Rachel and Josh who I could talk to, or laugh with, who understood the PK world we lived in.

Mom was the Rebbetzin (this is a term a Jewish congregation uses for the wife of a rabbi.) More than that, she was dad's full-time partner throughout his career as a rabbi. Sermon ideas, sermon rewrites, Temple programing ideas, Temple Sisterhood officer, substitute Hebrew school teacher, interim religious school director, and temple services logistics coordinator, mom did it all. Dad could not have done it without her. To be a rabbi was to give yourself and your time. To be a rabbi at a congregation of three thousand families was to give most, if not all of, your time. In addition to supporting dad, it was left to mom to also keep our family running – dealing with the homework, carpools, the dinners.

One last introductory note, if you are thinking this is a compilation of stories telling you how terrible it was to be a PK, or how resentful I was, it's not. To be sure, being a PK could be difficult and at times, and had its downsides (some of which I will share.) However, I loved my dad, I admired what he did, and I loved being a PK.

Does your Dad wear his robe and tallit when at home?

No joke, no made-up questions. All the questions in this book are real, and this is one I got a bunch of times growing up. Upon reflection, I guess it's a fair enough inquiry. After all, as little kids growing up in a synagogue, you would typically only see your rabbi on the bimah (the platform from which the rabbis and cantors conduct and lead services,) holding the Torah, reciting prayers, or telling stories from the Bible dressed in a robe and tallit.[1] That is the picture most of my friends had of my dad.

Sorry to disappoint, but usually my dad would trade in the robe for mismatched sweats or some type of jogging attire. My dad possessed a number of wonderful traits; however, fashion was not one of them. Comfort over style was his mantra. In his profession, there was no such thing as "business casual." Almost every day – including Saturdays and Sundays – he was in a dark suit and tie and dark, uncomfortable dress shoes, and not just for part of the day, but from morning until well after dinner on most nights. When it came time for services, performing all of those Bar and Bat Mitzvahs, weddings and funerals, it was a dark, heavy robe and tallit he would wear over his shirt and tie. So, when he hit home, it did not matter the color of the sweat shirt or the pants, he was just grateful to be out of that black suit and tie. It always took a new friend of mine a second to two (or three or four) to adjust when they would come over to my house for the first time and run into my dad, not in a robe or a dark suit, but in Nike or Adidas (or both.)

---

[1] You will notice the question is "robe and tallit" In our congregation our rabbis wore robes when officiating at services. A tallit is a Jewish prayer shawl that is worn over one's clothes during services. I did not forget to mention a kippah (a skull cap also worn by Jews while praying). In our synagogue the tradition for many years was for rabbis not to wear a kippah and wear only a robe or tallit. It was not until a few years after Dad became senior rabbi of the congregation that Rabbis (some, not all) wore a kippah long with their tallit.

One additional accessory dad often sported around the house was a dish towel. When he had the time, dad loved to cook (and he was a great cook.) It was typical to see him not only in the mismatched sweats, but with a dish towel over his shoulder as he prepared a family dinner in the kitchen. After the kind of hours he kept, his crazy schedule, I would think to myself, "Doesn't he want to lie down on the couch and close his eyes or zone out in front of the TV?" That, however, was not the Joseph Weinberg way. His relaxation and enjoyment came from hitting the kitchen and whipping up a special dinner with the dish towel firmly planted over the shoulder.

Did you have to go to Temple every Friday night?

And the award for the single most popular question a son of a Rabbi would get growing up is… Did you have to go to Temple every Friday night? The runner-up question does not come close to the number of times I got hit with this one. As I moved from elementary school to middle and then high school, the question continued to be asked, but was asked with a sense of impending horror or doom. It was asked with a sense of pity, "say it isn't so," for there was a party that Friday night or a high school football game.

"You're not going to be locked away in synagogue Friday night while the rest of us are running around from party to party, having a beer, and quickly fleeing once the cops show up are you?"

Looking back on this question, I notice that it was always phrased as "Friday night," not Saturday morning. It's a window into how Shabbat was viewed in our community growing up.

I did not go every Friday night, but I did go a lot, especially when I was younger. Temple was our family's dinner spot on Friday night. While other families might hit the Italian place around the corner, or the diner up the road, our family gathered at Massachusetts and Macomb Streets (the intersection in Northwest Washington, D.C. where WHC is located) many a Friday night growing up. When you have a father who was not home for dinner most nights of the week, and there was a kindergarten Shabbat dinner or the 4th grade Shabbat dinner or the Sisterhood Shabbat dinner, if we wanted to see dad, Temple is where you would find us, seated at a round table in Ring Hall (the name of the Temple's social hall,) with a platter of some type of chicken or brisket starring at us. At least they told us it was chicken or brisket. WHC had (and has today) many wonderful social action programs, classes, and services, but it was by no means a gourmet hotspot. When we were growing up, Temple employed an elderly woman who helped prepare the Shabbat dinners. She was an incredibly sweet person. She always had a big inviting smile and would always give a big hello and hug for Rachel, Josh, and me when she would see us at Temple. However, every time we saw her at Temple, she seemed to me missing another tooth. My brother Josh and I would often warn each other, "be careful when you bite into the brisket, you might find a tooth."

We did not go for the food. We went so the family could be together for Shabbat dinner.

Friday night dinner at Temple was followed by services which seemed very long. Mom would try to bribe us by saying, "After services, there will be wonderful dessert at the Oneg Shabbat[1]" (An Oneg Shabbat is a dessert reception held at the conclusion of Friday night Shabbat Services.)

Wonderful, it was not. Oneg Shabbat at WHC was ginger-ale and an orange sherbet concoction served out of some large silver punch bowl, and some brownies that tasted a little like they were left over from last week's Oneg, or the week before.

While the food and the dessert were far from Washington D.C.'s finest, it became part of our routine. Not only was it family time, it was in the course of these dinners and services that I really bonded with my brother and sister. After all, often times, it was just the three of us, mom, dad, and a room full of strangers. As we got older, we got to know many of them and form friendships with them, but at a young age, they all seemed very old, always patting us on the head, calling me Josh and calling Josh Jonathan. On the drive home from Temple the three of us would compare notes, "that lady was scary looking," "how old do you think she is?" We didn't gossip to be mean, and I think we were always nice when interacting with congregants, but there were some "unique" congregants out there.

When the brownies at the Oneg were particularly god awful, we convinced our parents to take us to Swenson's Ice Cream shop on Wisconsin Avenue, located close to the Temple. They have the best hot fudge sundaes around. Those Friday nights at Swenson's, hanging out after Temple, were so much fun. Ask Rachel or Josh, the best part of a Friday night at Temple, and I am confident they will go straight to the ice cream, hot fudge, whipped cream, and cherry on top.

On those Friday's when we were not at Temple, we always had Shabbat dinner at home before mom and dad would run to Temple for services. Mom would light the Sabbath candles and chant the blessing, Rachel would say a prayer over the Sabbath lights, I chanted Kiddush (the blessing over wine,) Dad would bless the children, and Josh blessed the Challah. Mom's chicken with some type of orange sauce was always on the menu, a step-up from the Temple brisket. These dinners were nice, but the clock was always ticking. If services started at 8:00, Mom and Dad needed to be out the door by 7:15. It took about twenty to twenty five minutes to drive to Temple, which left about fifteen to twenty minutes to prep for services. While we never raced through the meal, we were never able to sit and linger over dessert.

Growing up, our family's Shabbat routine did not end on Friday night, it extended into Saturday. Early Saturday morning, Dad would head out the door while Josh and I sat in our pajamas watching our Saturday morning cartoons. Saturdays for Dad were probably his busiest day of the week. On a typical Saturday, he would be out the door at 8:00 a.m. to get to Temple, where he would teach something called "Early Torah," or *ET*, a Torah study class that took place prior to Shabbat morning services at the Temple. After class, it was morning Shabbat services, which almost certainly included two B'nai Mitzvah. In the afternoon, it was often hospital visits, a baby naming, visiting a family who has just lost a loved one, and preparing for the funeral the next day. In the evening, he would be back at Temple for Havdalah services (the Jewish ceremony that separates the Sabbath from the rest of the week,) with another Bar Mitzvah. Often times, Havdalah services were followed by a dash to a downtown hotel to officiate at a wedding, only to come home late Saturday night and have to write the eulogy for the funeral the next morning. Saturday, the Sabbath, a day of rest? Not in Joe Weinberg's world.

However, in between the madness of his typical Saturday, we had our Shabbat lunches. At 12:30 on Saturday, mom and I would be in the yard gardening when Dad would pull into the driveway in his red sports car. (He always drove a red sports car. He started with a Mustang, followed by the Capri, and then the Honda Prelude.) He would pull into the driveway with the radio blaring "Live at the Metropolitan Opera." Out he would jump, holding two large

Sutton Place Gourmet or Giant Food shopping bags filled to the top. (Giant Food is the chain grocery store, while Sutton Place was the high-end grocery right around the corner from WHC that Dad frequented when we were growing up.) Mom would always complain about how much he would buy just for the five of us, but no matter, he would return the next week with just as much food for our Shabbat lunch feast.

The bags were always full of a variety of bagels, salads, and spreads, and we always had the most amazing chocolate-chip, heath bar crunch cookies for dessert. No Shabbat lunch was ever complete without these cookies. Sutton place has since gone out of business, and Giant doesn't make the cookies any more. I miss the cookies, and I miss the lunch.

As we got older, the Friday night Temple routine grew more infrequent, like most other teenagers, I could be found at the football games or riding around Potomac looking the for that Junior's house who we were told was having a party. Even if allowed out on Friday, mom and dad insisted that we try to have Shabbat dinner whenever possible, and most Friday's we still managed to be at the table together and receive our blessing from dad.

The fourth commandment says to honor the Sabbath and keep it holy. Growing up in the Weinberg household, Friday nights and Saturday were special. It was not so much a day of rest, certainly not for dad, but it was sacred in some ways. While there is nothing inherently "holy" about eating heath bar chocolate chips cookies on a Saturday, although I maintain it was close to a religious experience, the routine was special. The emphasis that family would be together at Temple on Friday night, or around our kitchen table on Saturday afternoon, that was special. During the week, like many other families, we all ran in our different directions. It was hard to get everyone together. Friday and Saturday, our family made sure we had time to sit together, to see each other, and to share with each other. In that way, I think we honored the Sabbath and kept it holy.

Does your dad curse?

It seems like a silly question, but it's one I would often get from my friends growing up. To my friends and acquaintances, they saw the rabbi standing in front of the ark, holding the Torah. The thought that a "man of God" could utter such words, it just did not fit their picture. The quick answer - shit, yes, he cursed. However, he was not a person to use curse words for the sake of cursing, Dad was laid back at home, not in the least bit high strung or prone to emotional outbursts laced with profanity. His gentle nature did not allow him to go that route. I do recall having a friend over, sitting on our deck for a brief timeout from our endless backyard football games. Dad was hammering at some nails on the deck when he hit his thumb. "Shit," he exclaimed.

"You OK dad?" I asked.

"I am fine," he replied.

I looked over at my friend, whose jaw had dropped and the water starting dripping from his mouth. He had a look of disbelief. Did he actually hear a "man of the cloth" just say the s-word?

The next day at the cafeteria lunch table. my friend regaled all of the others with the story

"Guys, I was at Weinberg's yesterday, and you will never guess what I heard..." The gang of ten-year-olds at the time seemed to think this was earth-shattering news. For me, it was my Dad who hit his thumb with a hammer and reacted like any one would Rabbi or non-Rabbi. But I let the group have its fun and smiled and laughed with the rest of them.

The topic of Rabbis and curse words reminds me of another story. In the 10th grade, I, like most other Jewish kids in our reform Temple, was in Confirmation Class. Confirmation is a post Bar Mitzvah ceremony in which boys and girls recommit themselves to Judaism. Unlike a Bar or Bat Mitzvah, which a child does on his or her own, Confirmation is a service in which an entire grade participates together. The entire year is spent learning together and the year ends with a special Confirmation Service at the Synagogue. In the months leading up to our formal Confirmation Service, the class of 100 students would gather in the sanctuary and go through many rehearsals for our service. These rehearsals lasted several hours. They were extremely boring and each and every person had to practice their part out loud on the bimah of the sanctuary.

Many kids would bring homework during these sessions, or read a book or magazine, or gossip back and forth waiting for their turn as the Rabbis asked for everyone to quiet down. One day, in the middle of a long session, it came time for a girl in our class to practice the poem she had written for the occasion. The other ninety-nine kids paid little attention. Dad was standing quietly next to her as she began to recite the first stanza of her poem. He stood next to everyone to help them along in their practice.

Dad whispered, in his most gentle voice, "a little louder."

Suddenly, she stops, wheels around to Dad, and at the top of her lungs, on the bimah in the sanctuary, in front of the Holy Ark, the Ark that contains the sacred Torah scrolls and yells, "FUCK! Will you stop talking to me?"

Ninety-nine sixteen-year-olds stopped dead in their tracks, the gossip ceased, all the heads buried in homework popped up. The silence that followed her outburst was deafening. Complete shock set in. Did this girl really just say that word to the rabbi in this place? More than one kid looked up at the ceiling. They had looks on their faces as if to say, *at any moment God is going to send down a thunderbolt to strike down this girl.*

All eyes turned to dad. Slowly and quietly, he just backed away, no comment, no lecture, no response (at least at that moment.) The girl turned back around and continued the recitation of her poem. Years later, whenever I see a classmate from my confirmation class, we still laugh at the time the rabbi got cursed out at Confirmation rehearsal.

One more story about rabbis and curse words.

"I did not know that rabbis knew that word," said the ninth grader as he met his parents after returning from a ninth grade weekend retreat.

Some quick background. Every year, our Temple would take the ninth graders on three weekend retreats during the fall, and three retreats for the eighth graders in the spring. This was a good deal. Instead of having to go to Hebrew School all semester long, we went on these three weekend retreats with all of our friends. Dad was the rabbi in charge of the program, so a few weekends a year, our entire family would head to Waynesboro, PA with Dad for these weekend retreats. The camp we often stayed at was called Camp Comet Trails.

Comet Trails had a one huge lodge that contained all of the bunks. Right smack in the middle of the lodge was a full length basketball court. Upstairs surrounding the court were six huge bunks where all the kids slept. These bunks formed a ring around the court. Downstairs, there were a few more bedrooms where our family would stay. It was all under one roof. Back to the story.

"What do you mean," asked the teen's father.

"You see, it was real early Saturday morning around 4:00 a.m. and I could not sleep. So, I went downstairs in the lodge to the basketball court. I started dribbling the ball and shooting at the hoop. Out comes Rabbi Weinberg in his pajamas, looks at me and says, 'Glen, what the fuck are you doing?'"

Did your Dad take you to sporting events?

I am a total and complete sports fanatic. I am not sure where my love or obsession with sports came from. My dad was much more of a casual fan. No matter the season, sports had my undivided attention, from the television, playing out my own sports season in our backyard, to reading every page of the Washington Post Sports page each morning, I loved sports (and still do.)

While I loved watching sports on television, getting the chance to actually go to games was little tougher. While our family lived comfortably, we lived on a rabbi's salary, so season tickets or frequent trips to a Redskins[2], Bullets (that's what they called our pro basketball team before they changed the name to the Wizards,) or Capitals games was not a possibility.

Salary and schedule did not deter my Dad. He knew of my passion and he made sure to get tickets whenever possible. Growing up getting a ticket to a Redskins game at RFK stadium was no easy task. These were hard tickets to come by. Imagine my delight as an eight year old when dad came home one night with the news of the year, a congregant had just given him two tickets to the Redskins game that Sunday. I would be going to my first live NFL game. However, as a PK, getting to my first NFL game would not be your typical experience.

The week crawled along until Sunday finally arrived. At 9:00 a.m., I was fully dressed and ready to go, sitting on our wooden bench by the front door. I had my sweatshirt, jacket, gloves, and even a burgandy and gold hat. I was actually not a real big Redskins fan, but the excitement of a pro football game live had me in the Redskins spirit. There I sat, waiting for my dad.

"Dad are you coming?" Finally, a few minutes later, my dad came down stairs. His attire? No, it was not the latest burgundy and gold parka, his attire… a black suit, black shoes, and some muted tie.

---

[2] Recently the Washington football team dropped this name. I use the term in a few places given that was the name of the team when I was growing up. It is not my intent to offend anyone by referring to the name of the football team at that time.

"Dad what in the world are you wearing? Aren't we going to the game? You're going to look like that at RFK Stadium?"

Both dad and mom assured me,

"Don't worry sweetie, of course you are going to the game," mom chimed in. "Daddy just needs to make a quick stop."

A few years ago, I was running to take my own son to a baseball game. I came home from work to pick him up and head down to the ballpark. Already a little late, I had no time to change and had to keep on my kakis and button down shirt.

"Dad?" Joey began to complain. "That is what you are wearing to the game? Nobody wears clothes like that to a ballgame." I had to laugh, remembering back, and my own dad's "black suit" game attire.

Off we went, Dad in his black suit and me in my "proper football attire," headed downtown toward the stadium. I was still a little confused by the back suit, but soon became excited as I caught a glimpse of Robert F. Kennedy Stadium (RFK) in the distance. No sooner had the stadium come into view, it started to fade away. We headed over the Anacostia River into Southeast Washington D.C.

"Dad" I began to protest.

"Just a quick thing I have to do and then we will be off to the game," he reassured me. Down a maze of side streets we went as dad navigated us. We turned on to Alabama Avenue and headed to a pair of large gates.

Washington Hebrew Congregation Memorial Park. The sign puzzled me.

A park, I thought to myself. *What are we doing here? What was this place?* The mystery and bewilderment quickly faded as the first tombstone came into full view. Then, more and more tombstones. Rows and rows and rows of dead people!

"The cemetery!" I cried out. "What in the world ware doing here? This is not RFK?" Dad quickly put the car in park, grabbed a black book, and opened his door.

"Jono, stay right here in the car. I will be back in a few minutes."

Before I could continue my protest, off he went in his black suit, his salt and pepper hair disappearing among the tombstones and over a hill. And then there was just me. Me, my football jacket, my gloves, my hat, sitting in the middle of a cemetery. I looked at the clock, kick-off time was fast approaching. It got very quiet. The only sound was the wind blowing the trees. What should I do? Dead people to the right, dead people to the left, all I wanted to do was get the game and have a hot dog. I sat in silence. A graveyard and an eight year old is not a good combination. I was a little scared, "freaked out," as my kids would say. Soon, my fear gave way to boredom and I started to read the tombstones. I devised a game, after all, that is what eight year-olds do. Could I find a last name on one of the markers that matched the same last name of a popular athlete? That did not last long. I was in a Jewish cemetery.

Next game, best tombstone in the place. I circled the view from the car to find the nicest I could find. There looked to be some "cool ones" over the hill, but I certainly was not getting out of the car in this place, and so that game to came to a quick end.

Next game, who is the oldest? Find the tombstone of the person who lived the longest life.

The game began searching through the rows and rows of tombstones. 1915 to 1950. Ouch. I was never a math whiz, but that poor guy only made it to 35. *That sucks*, I thought. The search continued. 1885 to 1971, ladies and gentlemen, we have a winner. That kept me entertained for a while, but soon I got bored. Kick-off time was inching closer and I was stuck next to Mr. and Mrs. Goldberg, "blessed husband and cherished wife," and they were not much for conversation.

Finally, some twenty or twenty-five minutes later, the black suit came back quickly walking over the hill.

"Told you it wouldn't be long."

Off we went, headed to the stadium. As we went along, dad peeled off his rabbi suit and into more suitable football attire. We were there for kick-off, like he promised. Sometimes, my friends would talk about the best pre-game party or tailgate they ever attended. While maybe not the best, but my tailgate at the WHC Memorial Park certainly ranks up there for most unique.

I was able to see my share of live games over the years. Besides my first NFL game, I could not have been more excited than the day dad came home with two tickets for the Oakland Raiders /Baltimore Colts play-off game. The Raiders were my team, and this would be the first time I got to see the Raiders in-person, and in a play-off game no less, I was thrilled.

That Friday afternoon, a serious issue arose. A congregant had the nerve to die and the family wanted dad to do the funeral that Sunday afternoon, the day of the Raiders play-off game. *People should really plan this "death stuff" better,* I remembered thinking to myself. This was one of the few times growing up I recall being a PK really bothered me. The playoffs, the Raiders, why couldn't my dad just have a normal, "run of the mill' job and we could go to the game.

Soon, my parents had the solution, mom would take me. God bless my mom! Off we went to Baltimore, Maryland and Memorial Stadium. Sunday was really cold. We found our seats surrounded by some of Baltimore's finest drunks, but there we were. I still vividly remember seeing the Raiders come out of the tunnel in their white shirts, silver pants, and silver helmets. As a young kid, there is nothing like getting to see it live and in-person.

The beer continued to flow up and down our section all afternoon long. The Colts' fans surrounding us taught me how to string several curse words together that, previous to that afternoon, I was unaware could be done. I am quite sure it was not mom's most fond experience, but we did witness what is still today called one of the greatest NFL games ever, with the Raiders winning in double overtime.

When we got home, I felt bad for my dad. One of the greatest games in the NFL history and he was stuck in a long black robe doing a funeral. However, as the evening went on, I provided a play-by-play recap. I could see he was happy; happy I had gotten the chance to see and experience the game. For dad, missing it was not a big deal, he was happy for me.

Did you have to go to Hebrew School every week?

"Where were you?" I asked my friends on a Sunday afternoon. "I was one of the only kids at Hebrew school today"

"We took the day off, "came the reply. "We can't go to Hebrew school every single week. Don't you get to skip once in a while?"

At that moment, I gave my friend a stare down.

"Have you forgotten who my dad is?"

While I would like to regale you with stories of how I managed to sneak out of Hebrew school, how when the teacher turned her back, we would make a run for it, or sneak out on our way to attend school services, but no such stories exist. Yes, you would find me at Hebrew school every week. I know, like every other Jewish kid I complained about it, but in my house, it was just me complaining, there was no dialogue on the issue, there was no discussion, I was going – end of story.

While my father was a more easy-going soul at home, it did not mean there were certain things he did not believe strongly in, and Jewish education and Jewish ritual were high on that list. On these subjects, he was not willing to yield. On Rosh Hashanah 1997, Dad gave a sermon which focused on the declining Jewish population in America, and the challenges as Jews became more and more secular. The last part of his sermon that night focused on attendance at religious school. After reading this expert, I think you will better appreciate where dad stood on the issue of Hebrew School attendance, and have a very clear answer to question above.

For many years, in our Religious School, we have made Bar and Bat Mitzvah contingent on an understanding that Religious School continues through Confirmation (Tenth Grade.) We ask our parents to make Judaism a priority in the lives of their children.

But in the last years, too often the phone rings and we hear,

"Jenny has decided not to go to Religious School any more. There are too many school pressures."

Another call,

"Michael has soccer, basketball, swimming, and lacrosse. I want a well-rounded child. Besides he's always going to be Jewish."

Can we really believe that Judaism on a sixth grade level will have meaning or staying power for a mature adult in the 21st century? If our twelve year old child tells us they are ending their religious education, we have to say, "that is not acceptable!" What if our child told us at the end of sixth grade that he was ending his secular education? No junior high, no high school, no college. It's a preposterous notion and we would not entertain the suggestion for a moment.

Of course we want our children to be well-rounded. But all activities are not equal and we have to set priorities. Probably the entire U.S. Olympic team will not be made up of Washington Hebrew Congregation! But I pray that all our children of WHC will make Judaism a dynamic living part of their lives.

And as we send our children off to religious school, let us remember that, if we want our children to remain Jews, then we have to make Judaism and Jewish learning a vital dimension of our very being. Judaism cannot skip a generation. It requires adults who will be role models for their children and grandchildren.

We have heard the dire predictions of demographers. But social scientists merely show us where the present trend will lead. They do not determine the future. That decision is ours.

Yes, I was at Hebrew school every week of every year.

Like every kid, I am sure I tried my best to get out of Hebrew School. Not like every kid, I am some unusual access.

I recall driving home one Saturday night with my parents from a Bar Mitzvah party. It started snowing quite hard. My parents began to discuss what to do about religious school the next morning. You see, unlike the public school system where the decision is made by some school superintendent or administrative operator, our religious school superintendent/headmaster/chief operations officer were all in the front seat of the car. What an opportunity to help out my fellow classmates. I weighed, with my twelve year old opinion, that I would be concerned having all those parents on the snowy roads. Canceling, I thought, would be the best option. I remember seeing my dad smirk at me through his rear view mirror,

"Jono, your concern for our congregants' safety is admirable." I can't recall if they actually canceled the next day. If they did, you are welcome to the hundreds of WHC kids that got a break from school that Sunday. If not, well, I tried my best.

How long was your Seder growing up?

Like several other questions in this book, there is a hidden (or not so hidden) message in the question. With a dad as a Rabbi, your Seder must take forever. (A Seder is the name of the service Jews conduct during the holiday of Passover. Unlike most Jewish holidays, a Seder is usually held at one's home, not at the Synagogue).

Our family's tradition was to have the first night of Passover at the Temple as part of the Congregational Seder. While all my friends would celebrate the holiday at home with family and close friends, our first night was celebrated with the congregational family (most years some 250 people.) It was a drill we got used to. After a few years, Rachel, Josh, and I could probably have run the Seder ourselves, as we were pretty good at memorizing the script.

Much like the Seder service, the meal that first night of Passover at Temple was also consistent. Consistently bad. It's hard to screw up matzo ball soup, but year after year they managed to do it. The matzah balls were like rocks. My siblings and I wondered if some of the silver-hairs would lose what remaining teeth they had trying to chew on those matzah balls.

A major highlight of any Seder is the chanting of the Four Questions. Sung in Hebrew, any pre-Bar or Bat Mitzvah child could be called upon to sing the Four Questions. At the Congregational Seder, it always fell on the Rabbi's kids to have to chant the four questions. As a nine or ten year-old, having to sing the four questions in front of a room full of people was daunting. I guess it was good practice for my Bar Mitzvah, at least that is what Dad told me as he informed me I was on "four question duty" for yet another year. No matter the number of times I had to chant the questions, the Four Questions performance scared me. Once we got past the Four Questions, I could relax and look forward to finding the afikomen. (The tradition at a Passover Seder is to take half a piece of matzah and hide it. The children, those under the age of Bar or Bat Mitzvah, would then go off to search for it, with the winner getting some sort of prize (a silver dollar was usually the big prize for the winner)).

The Congregational Seder was mostly attended by seniors. There were usually only a handful of families, so I liked my odds to find the afikomen. However, in all the years of these Congregational Seders, I never found the afikomen. Not once. That ticked me off then, and it still does to this day. You would think one of those years I would have come through. After all, no kid knows each and every crack and crevice of the Temple like me (or my siblings.) No matter, I never found that magical white napkin containing that elusive piece of matzah.

Certain years I tried to pump Michael Haberman for some inside information. Michael was the son of our, then, Senior Rabbi, Rabbi Joshua Haberman. At that time, he was in high school and had the responsibility for hiding the afikomen. You would have thought Michael would have given a fellow PK a break and provided a little hint, but he played it by the book – no hints, not even for a fellow Rabbi's son.

Night two of Passover was Seder at our home, this time not with two-hundred plus, but with our family, some family friends, and almost always with my grandma and grandpa from Chicago. Back to the question, *how long is your Seder?* Ask me when I was a kid and I would say it took forever; days, weeks. I never thought we would ever get to the matzah ball soup. You know, the part later in the Bible when the Children of Israel are wondering the desert for forty years before they reached Israel? As a young kid, I, too, felt our Seder service had us wondering through the desert and we would never reach the Promised Land, or in this case, dinner.

I remember sitting through the Seders and thinking, *this is taking even more time than it takes us to get our presents at Hanukah.*

Allow me to briefly jump to another Jewish holiday.

Like most Jewish families at Hanukah time, each night we would light the menorah and then chant the blessings. At most other houses, once you were done with the blessings it was… presents! Not at the Weinberg household. Finishing the blessings was just the start. My parents would then launch into Hanukah song after Hanukah song before you were able to tear into those tantalizing, gift wrapped boxes sitting on the table next the menorah. It was not merely one verse of *I Have A Little Dreidel*, these songs went on forever. If you think you have an exhaustive list of Hanukah songs, please contact me with your list. I assure you mine is longer.

Back to Passover.

As I got older, I understood better why the Seder "took so long." I realized what seemed like forty years was really not more than one hour. Passover, and in particular, the Seder, was one of Dad's absolute favorites. As a rabbi, he loved teaching. Seder was his private classroom, and he loved having his students all around him.

Each and every part of the Seder was exciting to him, and he was eager to share all of the stories and insights he had learned over the years. Second night of Passover was also relaxing. Unlike High Holiday dinners or Shabbat dinners, dad and mom did not have to jump up from the table and race to Temple. There was no place to go on the second night of Passover. It was a time to enjoy each other's company over wonderful holiday food, "Who Knows One," and Chad Gadya. Our Seder always concluded by listening to Martin Luther King's, "I Have a Dream". Dad did not read it, he wanted us to hear it. He would take out the record of "Great speeches of the 20th Century and place it on the record player so we could hear Dr. King's voice. (In a later chapter I will talk about the impact Martin Luther King Jr. had on my father's rabbinate.) Dad felt it was important that everyone at the Seder table not get up until each of us understood that the story of Passover and liberation from Egyptian slavery was not just ancient history, it continues today and we need to play a role in helping realize Dr. King's dream.

DOES YOU DAD REALLY BELIEVE IN GOD?

A friend of mine once inquired, "There is a lot of God talk during your dad's service. What's the deal? Does your dad really believe there is some old guy with a long gray beard up in the sky who controls our world? He can't really believe in God?" For some of my friends, the existence of a God was discussed at a similar level of "do you believe in Santa Claus?" Nice to believe in when you are young, but now that we are older, time to get real.

Dad believed in God. Dad's belief in God was strong. However, his belief in a God was not the old bearded guy in the sky. Dad had a much different view. What was his God?

He articulated it in a 1982 sermon, discussing Rabbi Harold Kushner's book, *When Bad Things Happen to Good People.*

> *What is the role of God? Where was God in Auschwitz? Where is he on a treacherous highway or in the intensive care unit? The answers become clear and the world's misery becomes so much more comprehensible if we stop imaging God as some kind of "cosmic superman" with x-ray vision, and unlimited power, "leaping tall buildings in a single bounce, snatching Lois Lane from the crashing Eiffel Tower and crushing deadly viruses whenever they appear. Nice work, Clark Kent!*
>
> *But it is only a movie, a fantasy, a fairy tale, wishful projection of a childlike yearning for a super powerful, loving protective parent. Alas it is not the real world.*
>
> *Our world does not evidence God as an independent conscious spirit. God is present, as the power or force of goodness in man. God does not do, God is not a person. But God is. God exists.*
>
> *God is the name we use for a power that is present everywhere in the universe, a power that is most especially present in man, the active*

image of God on earth. God is love, the capacity to sacrifice, the passion for justice, the ability to triumph over adversity. God is that productive, creative energy within us that inspires us to build a more compassionate society, to express human longing and ideals in music, art and poetry. God is that ever renewable and inexhaustible source of energy that brings goodness and loveliness into being. God is!

Who was the Rabbi at your Bar Mitzvah?

At the age of twelve and six months, while my friends would climb into the car with their parents and drive to begin working with their Hebrew tutors in preparation for their Bar or Bat Mitzvah, my tutor walked down the hall into my bedroom with the book containing my Torah portion in his hand. Was it strange or weird having my dad as my Bar Mitzvah tutor? What else did I know? This was my first Bar Mitzvah, so it seemed normal to me.

My friends often said,

"Oh God, he must have you practicing day and night"

"I bet you can't watch a second of T.V. until you have practiced at least three hours a day."

"He must be so hard on you if you make a mistake during practice."

The truth is, Dad was an amazing teacher, and he was far from a taskmaster. He was gentle, kind, unbelievably patient, and very encouraging. During each of our sessions, each verse or blessing ended with a "good," "great," or "Atta boy, Jono." He was so positive in working with me, especially when I was struggling. He was the perfect teacher… except for one little situation we encountered along the way to my Bar Mitzvah day.

I had been hard at work on my portion for two months. I still had about four months left before the big day. One evening, I was sitting in Dad's office in Temple, just prior to the start of Shabbat services. In walked Rabbi Steve Mason, one of the other rabbis at the Temple. Dad was busying shuffling papers around his desk, preparing for that night's service. Rabbi Mason started to talk to me about my preparation and my Bar Mitzvah date, when he realized the Torah portion for the weekend of my Bar Mitzvah would coincide exactly with the portion he had as a boy at his Bar Mitzvah. He was so excited. With that revelation, Rabbi Mason broke out into chanting the portion. He smiled joyfully, looking at me as he basked in the glow of remembering his special day. There was one issue. What the hell is this guy chanting? I did not recognize one single word. My dad lifted his head from his papers with a puzzled look.

"Um, dad," I stammered as Rabbi Mason continued to chant. "Could you tell me what Rabbi is saying, because that is not my portion."

At this moment, Rabbi Mason stopped. Seeing the bewildered look on our faces, he asked, "You don't recognize it?"

"I don't because it's not mine," I said.

Quickly, dad whipped out a Bible, Rabbi Mason swung around the other side of the desk, and they began to leaf through the pages.

"Dad," I said. "That's not my portion. It's nothing like my portion,"

"Jono, give us a minute," Dad replied as he and Rabbi Mason quietly conferred back and forth. I stood there frozen.

Finally, the two of them were done talking, and Dad smiled at me, "Jono," he said. "We have plenty of time, so it will not be a big deal, but I did assign you the wrong portion. The good news, Jono, this new portion is terrific. There is so much good stuff..."

It took me a few minutes to comprehend this. My dad, the Rabbi, the teacher, the tutor of all tutors, gave the wrong Torah portion to one of his students. Not just any student, but his son! After a few rough days, Dad and I were on to my new Torah portion.

The months leading up to my Bar Mitzvah were not easy. They were nerve racking and filled with pressure. I dreaded coming to Temple in those days, as countless silver-haired ladies would come up to me and say, "Are you ready? I am sure as a Rabbi's son, you will do great."

"Gee, thanks," I thought to myself. Nothing like putting a little pressure on a four and half foot, twelve year old with a singing voice that could summon dogs from all over the neighborhood.

Dad always reassured me, "Keep practicing and it will all be fine."

That summer, we took a family trip through Europe. I remember sitting in the front passenger seat of our rental car, driving through the Hungarian countryside, chanting away, with dad behind the wheel, and mom, Josh, and Rachel in the back. Hungry was still a communist country at the time, with a very small Jewish population. The sight and sounds of a twelve year old boy chanting Torah from the front seat of a Fiat, and we passed small village after small village is something that has stayed with me all these years later.

On Saturday morning, September 27, 1980, I became a Bar Mitzvah. Most, if not all, those silver-haired ladies were in attendance, as well as many others from the congregation. For all my nerves leading up to the day, by the time I was in front of the Torah, the jitters seemed to have subsided. My teacher had prepared me well.

To have my dad by my side not only as my dad, but as my rabbi, was incredibly special. Some fathers and sons bond over sports, or food, or over a television show, but for me, the months spent with my dad working together, sharing some laughs, working through feelings of self-doubt, and a "wrong portion" moment of terror, drew me closer to him. The feeling of having my rabbi, who also happens to be my dad, put his hands on my head and bless me is a moment that stays with me to this day.

Upon completing my portion, Dad lifted the Torah to show the scroll to the congregation. All of us on the bimah turned to the ark, away from the congregation, as dad lifted the Torah over his head. I looked over at Rabbi Mason, remembering that night in my dad's office four months ago. He smiled and shot me a thumbs up.

What was the theme of your Bar Mitzvah Party?

About six months shy of my daughter's Bat Mitzvah, amid all of the critical Bat Mitzvah issues, location of the party, color of the invitations, choice of DJ, what to serve, who to invite, what photographer, what florist, my daughter posed this question to me.

"So, Dad, what was the theme at your Bar Mitzvah party?"

"Well, Dani," I explained. "One would need to have had a party in order to have a theme"

My response sent shockwaves through her twelve year old body.

"No party? How is that even possible?

I began to explain my upbringing as PK, and what it meant when it came to a Bar Mitzvah party.

Let me start by saying we did in fact celebrate my Bar Mitzvah. I had lots of family from out of town travel to Washington, D.C. We had a family dinner at the Temple on the Friday night before my Bar Mitzvah. We had a big lunch for the entire congregation following the service in the Temple's social hall, and that night we hosted a dinner at our house for family. Celebrations, yes. The over-the-top, downtown hotel, DJ, dancers, empty your wallet party, no; we did not have that.

My parents were faced with a dilemma at all three of their children's Bar and Bat Mitzvahs. How could they throw a party and invite some of their friends, but exclude so many congregants? Would they not be hurting the feelings of countless people, who would feel snubbed they were not "good enough" to make the Rabbi's list? It was a real challenge (and I imagine it continues to be today for rabbinic families). The solution my parents came to was simply not to go down that path. Have a congregation wide lunch, invite everyone, and have the rest be just family. No big party, no theme. Lox and bagels, yes; fancy four course meal, no. Jewish folk music, yes; DJ with hip dancers, not at my Bar Mitzvah.

So how did I feel about all this? In writing this book, I thought back to my days on the "Bar and Bat Mitzvah circuit." (Bar Mitzvah circuit, when you are 12 or 13 years old, living in a large Jewish community, almost every weekend you are at another Bar or Bat Mitzvah party.) Surely I must have been resentful? I went to parties almost every week where another one of my friends got to have their moment in the sun – the bright lights, all the attention, a party just for them. Then, my day arrives and I get bagels and fiddlers. How did I feel? It did not really dawn on me that I was missing out, or somehow deprived in not getting a big party. You can say I am full of it; that any thirteen-year old would have resented their parents for not getting what all the others got. However, by the time I was thirteen, I knew I was different. Not in any special or conceded way, but because of who my dad was and our position in the congregation, my path, our family's route was simply different than those down the street.

My kids feel bad for me that I missed out on a big Bar Mitzvah party. I find that sweet. I told them in Jewish tradition, when a person reaches the age of 80 they get a second Bar Mitzvah. So, in approximately 30 years I will get another shot at a party, a theme, a DJ and dancers, mini-hot-dogs, and all.

Do you and your dad play sports together?

The real question behind the basic one is, are you allowed to play sports, or does your dad force you to sit inside and study the Torah day and night? When a new acquaintance would learn my dad was a Rabbi, I think their brain went to beards, long black coats, and heads buried in the Bible. That was not us.

My dad and I played lots of sports together. The types of sports evolved as I got older.

At a very early age, my brother, sister, and I had a favorite sport we loved to play with our dad. It was called "bed jumping." I was probably no more than five years old, making Josh three and Rachel eight or nine. We would be hanging around the house with dad when one of would call out "bed jumping," and up the three of us raced to our parents room, dad following closely behind. Each of us would take turns running from the top of the headboard and leaping into the air right at the foot of the mattress into Dad's arms. He would then toss us back on to the bed. We would laugh non-stop as the three of us flew through the air, back and forth from the arms of our dad and back on to the bad. While "bed jumping" is not an official Olympic sport yet, it was (and probably still is) the Weinberg children's favorite.

As I mentioned in a previous chapter, my father was not a huge sports fan, but no matter the season, I was always playing a sport. Given the central part that sports played in my life, Dad made sure to show interest so we could spend time together. Any trip to the beach included a baseball game with a plastic bat and whiffle ball. We played a fair amount of tennis growing up at our local community pool. Soon, I moved away from tennis and took up golf. My friends and I would often go over to the local golf course to play. Given my interest in this new sport, dad thought maybe he, too, would take a "swing" at it.

One Sunday morning, with his calendar clear, dad decided to hit the links with me. We brought along my younger brother, as he wanted to be part of this "guys outing." Soon, we were on the first tee at Falls Road Golf Course. As any golfer will tell you, the first tee is a frightening experience. The game is hard enough, but when you have twenty or thirty people all standing there watching you, the pressure is immense. It feels like you are on the first tee at The Masters. (While maybe not the Masters, it is nerve-racking). Josh was the first to hit. My recollection is he was about 8 or 9 years old, making me 10 or 11. Up he steps. Boom! He makes solid contact and hits it straight down the middle; the ball comes to rest about 125 yards from the tee box. Our onlookers seemed impressed with the young kid. Next, I get up. Bam! I hit one of the best drives of my life. The ball goes about 175 yards, right in the middle of the fairway. Now we have our gallery's attention, you can hear what they are saying,

"Wow these two little kids are good for their age, dad must be really good and taught them well."

Up steps dad, who probably only played golf one other time in his life, but the crowd watching did not know this fact. A mighty swing and… Bonk! A feeble little dribbler of a shot, barely making it off the tee box. Dad was less than pleased and slightly embarrassed. The rest of the round didn't go much better for Dad. He always seemed to connect with his congregation when it came time for a sermon, but connecting with the little white golf ball that morning seemed to be a challenge.

We finished our round and dad said, "Boys, I am so happy you enjoy the game, have fun playing, but I think it's for the birds."

That was the last time Joe Weinberg ever set foot on a golf course.

Like most other dads, we would, from time to time, come out to the yard to throw a ball or two. One Saturday afternoon, after building our Sukkah (a Sukkah is an open-air canopy like structure Jews erect during the holiday of Sukkot in the fall) Dad and I went to the yard for a game of one on one touch football. As we played, it started to rain. Dad called hike, I charged after him, he faked one way and went the other, and then… Down he went in a heap, and in a ton of pain. Mom came running out. I felt terrible.

"I didn't touch him, honest," I pleaded.

An hour later, we were in the emergency room at Holy Cross Hospital on a Saturday afternoon with dad getting a cast for his broken leg. He was the only one in the ER that afternoon who was over the age of seventeen and who was not wearing a high school football uniform.

From then on, we did not play a whole lot of outdoor sports, but we did have fantastic chess matches. And the only time I was locked away to "study Torah" was for a few days prior to my Bar Mitzvah.

DOES YOUR DAD GET NERVOUS UP THERE?

This was a popular question I got around age thirteen, more specifically, age thirteen right after a friend just had their Bar or Bat Mitzvah.

"Jonathan, does your dad get nervous when he is conducting services or giving a speech?" they would ask. "During my Bar Mitzvah I felt like I was going to pass out when I was up there"

It is a question I once posed to my dad.

"It's my job, it's what I do every week and it comes with the territory, so no, I am not really nervous when I am conducting services."

The answer seemed logical to me. I was ready to accept it and move on when he amended his answer. "High Holidays. I get a little nervous during the high holidays."

As a big sports fan, let me to try to explain the High Holidays (Rosh Hashanah and Yom Kippur, the two most important holidays in the Jewish year.) Think Super Bowl; think World Series; think Final Four. While I would like to say the ten thousand members of Washington Hebrew Congregation were regular attendees at services on a weekly basis, it quite simply was not the case. A large majority of congregants only turned out twice a year; Rosh Hashanah and Yom Kippur.

So, while Dad could be doing a terrific job as a Rabbi all year long, organizing wonderful social action programs, performing all sorts of special life cycle events, and ministering to those in need, for a large chunk of the WHC "faithful," their only exposure to the rabbi was the sermon at the High Holidays, and that is in large part how he would be judged. No pressure, right?

My dad's preparation for his High Holiday sermons began in early August, usually during a trip to the beach. Mom and Dad would start to discuss topics. Dad would have five or six books around with all sorts of book marks in each one. Then, he would lock himself in his study for hours. Growing up, we did not have many strict rules or chores at our home, but a few weeks prior to the High Holidays, when the study door was closed, we knew and observed the golden rules. Keep quiet. Do not disturb. Steer clear of the study.

He would write, and mom would read. He would rewrite, and mom would re-read. This was a back and forth that would take place for several weeks, when, finally, the sermon was a finished product. Dad's secretary would type it up, hand it to him, and again he would disappear into his study and begin his practice. For dad, the words on the page were only half the battle. He wanted to make sure he delivered the sermon the best he could, and that meant lots and lots of practice.

Dad would prepare right up to "kick-off." As soon as I was able to drive, I would be the one to drive dad down to Temple on the High Holidays after our holiday dinner. Dad would get into the passenger seat with a small tape recorder glued to his ear. He taped his sermons and would listen to it on the days leading up to services as another way to become as familiar as possible with the text. This allowed him to be "freed up" on the pulpit, to make eye contact, and to fully "preach," not just read his sermon.

Always, he asked me the same question on the way down.

"Jono, is this bothering you? I can turn the volume down. Are you sure?"

This was typical Dad. Moments away from the biggest night of his professional year and he was worried the tape recording of this sermon was bothersome to me. It never did, and I loved those drives with my Dad. While I did not talk to him much, for I wanted him to concentrate on his preparation, I felt close to my dad as we headed down Massachusetts Avenue to High Holiday services. I also loved arriving with my dad and walking with him from the parking lot to his study. Each and every person wanted to say hello to dad, to wish him a happy new year, to get or give a hug. To see so many, one after another, show such an outpouring of love and affection, I knew and learned just what a special person dad was in the lives of so many, and how lucky I was to have him as my father.

When Dad became the Senior Rabbi, he delivered the sermons on both Rosh Hashanah and Yom Kippur eve (called Kol Nidre.) Given the size of WHC, we had two services on each holiday eve, an early service starting at

6:00 p.m. and a late service starting at 8:45 p.m., to accommodate the number of congregants. On Rosh Hashanah, in between the early and late service, the Temple had a tray of fruit and cookies brought to the Senior Rabbi's study, where the rabbis, cantor, and their families could spend a little down time in between the services. (Many a time, I longed for the tray in between Yom Kippur services, but something about a fast got in the way of that plan). I loved this tradition growing up. It was not that the cookies were so good, it was a rare social moment between the clergy, their spouses, and PKs. There were not many times during the year this group would all be in one place to share a few moments together. I vividly remember, when I was young, how intimidated I was to go into the office of then Senior Rabbi Haberman. After all, he was the chief of the chief, the top of the top. Rabbi Haberman, who was probably only 5 feet 3 or 4 inches tall, was, nonetheless, a large presence. Our dad was just the junior rabbi and I wondered as little kid, *Are the cookies meant for the kids of the junior rabbi?*

I remember Josh and I hanging near the door of Rabbi Haberman's study, eying the cookies when he spotted us, "Come in boys," he boomed. "Don't let the cookies go to waste."

Rabbi Haberman may have been intimidating to a young kid, but he was always warm and welcoming to our family.

The cookie tray get together also served as a "halftime." Dad was always a little anxious about how he did in the first service.

"Was it OK?" he would ask.

I never remember having to sugarcoat or lie to dad during any of those "halftimes." Of course I was biased, but I thought he was always great. I knew the tremendous time and effort he (and mom) poured into this moment, and I was so very proud to be his son at those moments. From time to time, others would come into the office to greet Dad and the other clergy. It never got old watching people embrace dad, telling him how moved they were or how inspired he made them feel that night. While I am sure there are some that did care for what he had to say, "too long," or "too political," my memories of Dad's Super Bowl/World Series/Final Four were all winning moments.

Did you play sports in high school? Was your dad able to attend?

As I entered high school, I joined the wrestling team. No, dad did not take up wrestling, although we used to have great wrestling matches with him on my parents' bed, as I previously mentioned. Maybe that is where I developed the interest in the sport – flying off the bed into his arms, and tossed back into a sea of pillows.

I clearly remember my first high school wrestling match at Churchill High School with both mom and dad in attendance. I was elated to have won, and when I got home dad shared in my joy, asking for a minute by minute replay of the match.

"Where is mom?" I asked.

"She is upstairs, not feeling to well," dad replied.

I later learned that seeing her son pulled and twisted in various unnatural directions on the wrestling mat was too much for mom. She promptly came home from that first match and threw-up.

"I love you sweetie," she would say. "But from now on, just your father will be going to your matches."

And that was the way it was for the rest of my high school wrestling experience. Dad's schedule did not allow him to get to all the matches, but he went out of his way to attend a lot of them. Of course, he almost always attended in his black suit and tie, as he was typically running between appointments. While the rest of the crowd was clad in the blue and green, the colors of my school, dad was usually "suited up." His attire did not take away from his enthusiasm. My memories of my wrestling matches are two – a big blur and my dad's voice.

As a kid who wore glasses throughout high school, wrestling did not exactly allow you to keep your glasses on while some other teenager tried to take your head off. (Contacts could have solved this problem, but I did not make that switch until college). So, when it was match time, off came the glasses. I have really bad eyesight, so while I could see my opponent right in front of me, the rest of the picture was a blur – the crowd, the scoreboard, even my coach and teammates on the bench. Because I could not make out the numbers of the scoreboard, my teammates had to yell out the score during the match.

While my vision was not real good, my hearing was fine, and I always heard one voice loud (really loud,) and clear. Dad. From the opening whistle to the end, I always heard him in the familiar, "Come on Jono! Way to go! Great job!"

He was always encouraging, and never over the top. It is dad's voice that is the soundtrack of my memories of high school wrestling.

At the conclusion of my match, he would come down from the stands and talk to me for a few minutes behind the bench. He often needed to run to his next appointment, but he wanted to tell me in-person how proud he was of me.

My kids attended Churchill High School. I remember going to a football game a few years ago and seeing them sell t-shirts with a big Superman "S" on the chest, with a banner below that read *Churchill Super Fan*. That was Dad for me. He probably would have liked the shirt a lot better than his traditional black suit, as well.

Are there any perks to being a Rabbi's Kid?

I hope I have articulated through much of this book how much I loved my dad, how proud I was (and still am) to be his son, and how I would never have changed places with anyone in the world. In that way, being the son of Joe Weinberg was one huge "perk." However, the question was less about my overall experience, and more day-to-day focused. We did get great seats for services, close to the front with a great view. I know, in the world of "perks," probably not high on the list. Several years ago, catching up with a high school friend of mine, and recounting our senior year at Churchill High School, I was reminded of one amusing advantage to having your dad as a rabbi.

Like most seventeen and eighteen year high school seniors living in the suburbs of Washington D.C., a popular destination on the weekends was to head downtown, especially to the bars in Georgetown. At the time, Maryland's drinking age was twenty-one, however, the drinking age for the District of Columbia – a mere twenty minute drive – was eighteen at the time. That made the bars in Georgetown a favorite and frequent destination. There was one major obstacle to overcome, however, each and every weekend, and that was the nightmare of parking in Georgetown. Georgetown had great bars, places to eat, lots of shops, and was filled with tourists, college kids, and yes, a bunch of high school kids. However, Georgetown had absolutely no place to park your car. Typically, my friends and I would trade-off who was our designated driver, and with that job came the unenviable task of trying to find a spot on the jammed neighborhood streets of Georgetown. Like everyone else, I took my turn, dreading the parking situation. On a Saturday night, while sitting in my Dad's red Honda Prelude, with a friend next to me in the passenger seat and three others jammed in the back, stuck in bumper to bumper traffic as we entered Georgetown, I discovered a most intriguing piece of laminated paper stashed on the driver's side pocket door. On one side, it read

"Clergy Emergency," and on the other, "Clergy Official Business." This could be a game changer. Dad's business often took him to places where he was in a rush to see a congregant in need, usually this was around a hospital, but there were other situations, as well, which required him to get to where he was going quickly, without having to search for a parking spot. I am not sure if the sign was issued by the Temple, or if the rabbinic association provided it. All I knew at the time of discovery was it looked very official. Very official and very enticing.

At first, I was a little hesitant and scared, but after some gentle, (well, not so gentle,) persuasion from my friends and a continual frustrating search for a space, I gave in. I swung the Prelude into a clearly marked "No Parking" space, put the car in park, and put my Clergy Emergency sign on the dash. Off we went to Winston's (my favorite bar in Georgetown, given I had a crush on one of the waitresses.) A few hours later, the moment of truth arrived. Did it work? Were the police going to be waiting for us? Was the head of the Washington Rabbinical Association going to be there? Was he going to be there with my dad? Sweat began to form on my forehead. Had I pushed the envelope too far?

Up the street we walked, breathing hard, and then the moment of truth. There sat the Honda Preclude, still in the spot, surrounded by no one, no boot on a wheel, no ticket on the window shield. Success! We were elated.

As the weeks progressed through that senior year, dad's Clergy Emergency sign worked like a charm. Even when I was not the DD, my friends would greet me as they came to pick me up:

"Do you have it?"

"Nice to see you guys, too. Yes, I have it."

While great seats at the Temple for Rosh Hashanah or Yom Kippur services may not be considered to many as a "perk," if you needed parking in Georgetown on a crowded Saturday night, I was your man, or should I say, dad was the man. I was just lucky enough to discover the "magic" parking pass.

Did you feel extra responsibility or pressure as a PK?

There were certainly times growing up as a PK I felt there was some added pressure, or additional responsibility put on my shoulders. My Bar Mitzvah, having to recite the Four Questions at the Congregational Seder, were what I would call "performance pressures." We had to do something in front of a large group, and they expected us to do it very well, given who our father was.

From time to time, I felt other types of pressure, especially at Hebrew School or Temple youth group activities. Once, when my entire Hebrew School classed flunked an exam, including me, the teacher lectured the class and concluded with, "And Yonaton (my Hebrew name,) I am so surprised at you, after all your father is the rabbi, and there is no excuse for you to fail." Footnote to this story, Dad had a little discussion with the teacher after I told my parents what she said, and the next week the teacher apologized to me.

As a PK there were certain "responsibilities" we had or more accurately things that "came with the job." When there was a special service or an important milestone in the life of our synagogue, it was expected that the Rabbi's family would be in attendance. There were other less formal occasions that were also part of the PK routine. Every summer a small group of seniors would host my mom, Rachel, Josh, and me for an annual lunch, tuna fish sandwiches always on the menu (still today once of the best tuna sandwiches around, diced apples mixed in the with tuna was the key!).

I did not feel an overwhelming sense of responsibility to be a "model citizen" growing up. I cut school, and yes, sometimes I did run into someone from the Congregation when I should have been in my fourth period English class. Yes, I did drink with the rest of my friends in high school. I never felt, because my father was Rabbi Weinberg, that I should not be doing the typical teenager stuff. However, there is some additional responsibility that was put on us. At times, it meant growing up a little faster, or dealing with death or disease at an earlier age because that was part of our dad's everyday job and, hence, part of life in our home. Mom and Dad never lectured on the need to set an example (with maybe one or two exceptions) but through certain experiences, they did put us in positions of needing to grow up a little faster and deal with a little more than other kids.

It was the summer of 1982 and, as with many summers growing up, our family was on a Congregational trip to Israel. However, this journey was different, as Israel was in the midst of a war in Lebanon. One evening, Mom and Dad called Josh and I into their room (Rachel was home for that trip, as she had an internship at the White House that summer.) Our parents explained they had been asked by the IDF (The Israeli Defense Force) to go into Lebanon and witness IDF operations; to actually witness the war. That summer, Israel had taken a beating in the press. Article after article and report after report took Israel to task, painting an ugly picture, claiming Israel was indiscriminately bombing civilian targets. The Israeli government knew this to be not only unfair, but also wholly inaccurate. They believed if American Jewish leaders could see firsthand how Israel took great pains to use extreme care and caution not to harm innocent civilians, these leaders could begin to right the wrongs in the press back home. Mom and Dad were selected by the IDF to go into Lebanon.

Our parents explained they would leave early in the morning and be back late that same night. They asked us not to let the tour group know where they were headed. They wanted the group to enjoy that day's sites and not be worrying or thinking about them. They said we should also help out Ezra, our tour guide. We questioned them about safety, but they assured us they would be fine and would be back with us in no time.

This was a lot to put on a fifteen and a thirteen year-old. Josh and I were scared. Our parents were headed into a war zone. But, we also knew this stuff came with the job. It was a "quick grow-up moment."

The next day was long. Mom and Dad left our hotel at 4:00 a.m., kissing our heads as they exited the room, leaving Josh and I alone. At breakfast, we told the group mom and dad were in Tel Aviv planning an end of tour celebration. Throughout the day, adults and kids from our trip quizzed us on the party details. We continued with the charade,

"We promised our parents we would not give any of the details."

"It's going to be a great celebration," we told them.

The day dragged on. On the outside, we put on a fake smile, on the inside, we were scared for our parents and for us. Were our parents safe? Finally, late that night, our parents returned to the hotel. They had incredible stories to tell, which they did with our group the next day, and with many media outlets upon returning home to the United States.

In most cases, I like to think we handled the role of PK and the extra responsibility well. However, that was not always the case.

Did you ever let your dad down?

I honestly believe just once. If there were other times, he kept it to himself. He was always encouraging, supportive, and gentle. That being said, I do know one time I let him down, not just as a PK, but as his son.

It was my second semester of my senior year in high school. As any kid who has lived through these months, you know well, senior year second semester is one long party. Most of us were into college, high school was already in our rear view mirror, and having fun and partying it up with our friends was the sole priority.

In February, our Temple Youth Group planned its annual ski trip to Killington Vermont. As President of the Youth Group, I was involved in setting up the trip. However, in the weeks leading up to the trip, I wore another hat than that of Rabbi's son who is the synagogue youth group leader. I was chief party planner. My friends and I were determined to make the Killington trip a senior year highlight. We began our preparations weeks in advance. "Preparation" was not what to pack, meaning how many sweaters or hats, rather, our planning was surrounded by how much alcohol we could stash away in our bags for the trip.

Two days before our trip, our home phone rang late at night. The ring of the phone in our house growing up after 9:30 or 10:00 sounded more like an alarm bell – it almost always meant bad news. After a brief conversation, dad sprinted out of the house into his car and sped off. The next morning, I would learn a teenager in the congregation had died that night. It was an unbelievable tragedy, and the entire community was in shock. Even though this was a terrible tragedy, the ski trip would go on as planned the next day.

Before I left, mom and dad pulled me aside and said, "Please be good this weekend, we are going through a lot here and we need for you to be responsible."

I would like to say I didn't hear them. I would like to say I misunderstood their message. But their words were clear and I knew what the next few days would be for them. For the most part, growing up as the son of a Rabbi, I think I knew I had some extra responsibility and I was viewed a little bit different than the kid down the block. I think most times I acted appropriately and responsibly. However, this time I did not. I nodded that I had heard them, but grabbed my bag full of alcohol and boarded the bus and headed to Vermont. At that moment, I choose to be a 17 year-old high school senior, not a Rabbi's kid, and not President of the Youth Group.

The ski trip started off really well, and then took a turn for the worse. We had our share of drinks, providing them to many others on the trip (most of whom were juniors, sophomores and, yes, even some freshman.) The party was a blast, until we got caught by the chaperones.

"I am going to have to report this to your dad," the lead chaperone said, "I will also have to let him know of all the other kids"

I told him I understood. He was a family friend, but also an employee of the Temple and I could not expect him to look the other way with kids drinking on a Temple sponsored trip.

The bus pulled back into Potomac on Sunday night, with my parents waiting in the parking lot. They had just concluded several days of agony, a funeral for a young boy, and the impossible task of comforting his family and friends. Now, it was late Sunday night and they were meeting the youth group bus with reports of widespread drinking of all the kids, including their son.

Dad was not a big speech giver at home, mom took on that role, and that was the case when we got home that night. I could see the look on dad's face – he was supremely disappointed, but he did not say a word. Mom laid into me, a tongue lashing that was more than well-deserved. The next day, dad still was not speaking to me. Later the next night, I remember him coming into my room. He spoke calmly.

"Do you know what I have been doing tonight" he asked. "I am having to call the parents of each kid who was caught drinking on the trip. And do know what they say to me? '"Rabbi, my son said that they got the beer from the

Rabbi's son,' 'Rabbi, my daughter said it was your own son who was serving the drinks'."

He continued to stare me down. I apologized, and let him know how disappointed I was in myself and was sorry for the embarrassment I caused him. I think he wanted to lay into me more, but I think hearing the word "embarrassment" dad let up. I think he understood that 17-year-olds do really dumb things. Even a seventeen year old PK was not immune from that type of behavior.

My dad and I sat on my bed and spoke for a while about teenage pressures and about choices. After a while, we agreed we would move on from this. He got up, gave me a hug, and headed for the door. My parents grounded me for two weeks. All in all, it was probably a more than fair punishment.

The look on my father's face during that time is something I can still see today. As I deal with my own kids now, I am reminded of the ski trip, of making poor choices, talking with my children and trying to get them to understand the consequences of their choices. To be sure, being a parent means being disappointed in your kids from time to time. It also means understanding they are kids, they will fall down, and I need to pick them up and move on.

How long is your Dad's sermon tonight?

A close family friend had a long-standing tradition when it came to the High Holidays. Each family member would throw a few dollars in the pot and would guess how many minutes the Rabbi's sermon would be that night. The one who was the closest would win the money. I know what you are thinking, gambling on the Rabbi? And on the holiest of holidays? However, this was a long-standing tradition, and Judaism is a religion based on tradition and bringing the family together, and this checked both boxes.

One of the brothers in the family got smart one year. As I was growing into a young teenager, he figured he would "pump" the PK for inside information and see what he knows. I was not much help, as I was out of the loop on sermon timing issues. However, the inquiry that year did tip me off to the pool. As a sports fan, and liking to bet with my friends, I wanted in on the "action." So, the next year, they let me in the High Holiday sermon pool. Now that I was part of the group, it was time for me to do some "recon."

"Mom" I innocently inquired, "how long are dad's normal sermons when it's not the high holidays? And are his sermons longer for the holidays because they are so special?"

Not knowing I would eventually go into the practice of law, I already had a knack for leading the witness in just the right direction in order to extract the information I was looking for. After getting my mom to give me an idea of how long (she never knew why I asked,) I submitted my entry into the pool. You will never guess who won that year. You will never guess who has banned from ever participating in the betting pool after that year because he was "an insider."

There is one additional fact about the High Holiday sermon pool. The winner of the pool each year would take the money and contribute it to the Temple. Not such a sacrilegious practice after all.

Are your Dad's sermons ever about current events?

Upon graduation from high school, I headed off to Madison, Wisconsin and the University of Wisconsin. My college experience was fantastic, but, like every incoming freshman, there is always a little bit of homesickness. To my surprise, the first time I really missed home was not a family member's birthday or some anniversary, rather, it was my first High Holidays away from home. It was first time I was away from my dad, my family, and WHC. I had grown accustomed to our routine at home and, most of all, I had grown-up watching my dad on the pulpit preaching sermons. This would not be the case in Madison that fall.

I still wanted to attend services that first year away and, while most of my Jewish friends went to Hillel, a few of us managed to get tickets at the local reform synagogue in Madison. That is where I found myself on Rosh Hashanah eve.

This was not my father's congregation. The music seemed strange, the surroundings unfamiliar, and, most of all, the sermon was not what I was used to. Headed back to campus that night, a friend asked me what I thought of the sermon,

"C minus," I replied.

"Man you are harsh," he replied. "It wasn't so bad."

"He didn't say anything, he didn't take on any of the issues of the day," I replied. My friends looked puzzled and confused.

"What do you mean?" they asked. "A rabbi's talk has nothing to do with current events. They talk about the Torah portion for that week and tell us a few Jewish stories, stuff like that."

Seeing my puzzled look, they would ask me the question,

"Does your dad get up there and talk about current events?"

Central to my father's rabbinate was the belief to stand-up for what you believe in. Be it a new social action project he thought Temple should participate in, or telling the President of the United States he is wrong, dad spoke his mind. There was no-back down in Joseph Weinberg. Not everyone liked or agreed with it. There were plenty of conversations I overheard, "why is the rabbi being so political" that it "was not his place." But that never deterred dad from speaking what he thought needed to be said. I think he felt a special obligation to weigh in on the issues of the day, given our congregation was located in Washington, DC, the most powerful city in the world and, often times, with powerful and influential policymakers sitting in its sanctuary.

What were the issues he cared about and what did he have to say on them? The following are experts of sermons in which dad addressed current national and world events.

> JUNE 1970 '(Dad had only been at WHC for two years when he gave this sermon. He was the junior rabbi and was 33 years old.)
>
> *Only a few short years ago we were told by our leaders that eighteen year old boys had to go and die in Vietnam to protect the freedom of the South Vietnamese, and more importantly because our own security was imperiled. The Secretary of State gave us a choice between stopping the Viet Cong in Saigon or at Chevy Chase circle (a traffic circle nearby our Temple).*
>
> *How dreadful that it has taken a death toll of more than 50,000 Americans and untold Vietnamese and five years of elusive victories to bring our nation to its senses. The majority of our people now feel that we should have never gotten involved in the first place but now that we are there we cannot withdraw precipitously.*
>
> *What an obscenity of obscenities! Now they admit their error! Where were you when we needed your courageous conviction before the corpses come home for the last time? Where were you when we were asked to exchange cap and gown for fatigues and boots? Where were you when we were asked to exchange summers in the country for forever in a rice paddy grave? Where were you when they said 10,000 men no more, 50,000 men no more, 100,000 men and more and more and more. Where were you?*

December 1973

We have lost confidence in our President. We simply do not believe him anymore. Whether we liked Mr. Nixon's programs and policies or not, the lack of trust and credibility is a national calamity. It is time for us as Americans to stand up and demand that we be given a government and a leader in whom we can believe.

It is time for us to stand up and say enough. It is time for us to demand the truth. Too long have we permitted government by deception to be the standard operating procedure for our elected leaders. Too long have we accepted administration by manipulation. To long have we allowed the distortions and lies of the highest officials to be passed off as "misspoken words" instead of deliberately contrived mendacity.

For all of us who love this country dearly, it is a time of great national sorrow, but it must, if we are to redeem ourselves from the mire of the past, also be a time of truth. Mr. Nixon can perform his greatest service yet to America and I say this with profound sadness, if he would step aside and allow the nation new national leadership.

October 1980

If we are to safeguard our freedoms and preserve the American way of life which has given us the opportunity to flourish, then Jews and Christians of good will must join hands (as we have done so often in the past) to preserve and protect the separation of church and state.

September 1985

Apartheid is a cruel and inhuman suppression of twenty-five million people, solely because they have black skin. Apartheid means social degradation, illiteracy, isolation, capricious and forced resettlement. In the last decade, four and a half million blacks have been driven into desolate "homelands" barren wasteland, hundreds of miles from urban centers, with few schools and jobs and little food, water, or medical care. Thousands have been jailed and over 600 have died in the escalating violence.

Again and again we have heard the Foreign Minister Pik Botha ask the world and South African blacks to be patient. We hear empty promises, meetings with black leaders that never take place, better social conditions that only become worse, and legislative representation and meaningful black participation in government that never takes place. Gradual reform is not what is needed. As Bishop Desmond Tutu recently declared, "We don't want apartheid liberalized, we want it dismantled. You cannot improve something that is intrinsically evil."

FEBRUARY 1988

The shots ring out day and night. There are blood curdling screams, human life crushed, crumbles, falls amidst the rubble, the dreams of tomorrow, the hope of the future is snuffed out, obliterated in an instant. Youth that will never know maturity.

The West Bank? Gaza? Soweto?

No! These are not scenes of distant violence and conflict, they are daily portraits on the streets of the Nation's Capital, Washington, D.C., the capital of the free world. For just over two months we have witnessed a growing and increasingly explosive terror of murder and gangland type assassination.

Every single day, the mindless killing of a new kind of war is described in the morning press and evening news. All of this is happening just down the street, a few minutes from our homes and places of work, in our own back yard.

SEPTEMBER 1993

It was almost impossible at first to comprehend what was happening. Just two days ago I sat together with Arabs and Jews, members of Congress and the Cabinet in the Rose Garden of the White House and watched along with millions around the world in hopeful anticipation, as Shimon Peres and Mahmoud Abbas signed the peace accords and then Prime Minister Yitzhak Rabin and Chairman Yasser Arafat shook hands. Can it really be?

Is your Dad a good driver?

This is not what I would call a standard PK question, rather, its specific to Joe Weinberg and his driving "skills." I remember getting the question once, in the context of a friend who happened to be on the road and saw my dad "weaving in and out traffic like he was late for services." Driving with dad could be an interesting experience, especially if we were headed to Temple and he was running a little behind schedule.

There were countless occasions when I was younger that I would be waiting for dad as we were headed to Temple for services, a dinner, or a Temple program. I would be fully dressed, standing at our front door, ready to go. Before he would actually appear, you could get a whiff that he was approaching. Dad was a Brut man. I don't mean a "brut" like some strong, hulking man, I mean Brut the after shower cologne found in a green bottle. I believe the proper name is Brut 33. I think the stuff is just meant to dap a little bit here and there. Not in Dad's case. He would dump that green bottle all over himself. Mom would say, "Joseph! Enough!"

So, as I waited patiently for him to appear, I could catch a little whiff of that magic green bottle and knew he was on his way. Dad would come bounding down the stairs, dress shirt fully open, tie dangling from his shirt, belt in his hand, and suit jacket in the other, hair wet, and not combed.

"Ready, Jono," he would say.

"Is that how you are showing up at Temple?" I would ask.

"Of course not, I will finish getting dressed on our way," he would say. Then, the fun began.

Our route from Potomac, Maryland to Northwest DC took us about twenty minutes to navigate through several different roads. One road on the journey is particularly distinctive. Seven Locks Road.

Seven Locks is hilly; up and down the entire way. Seven Locks also has constant sharp turns that swing violently from left to right and back again.

The road required both hands on the wheel... Well, at least for some of us. As we headed down Seven Locks, dad would take his hands off the wheel and would start to steer the car with his knees. *His knees*. It was time for him to finish getting dressed.

The rabbi could not show up with an open shirt and no tie, and so our commute to Temple would be the place he would finish getting dressed. Down the road we went, knees with a quick touch of the wheel from time to time, sliding his belt through the loops in his pants, buttoning his shirt, tying his tie, putting on his cufflinks, and combing his hair as he looked back and forth in the rear view mirror. As we got closer to Temple, our route required us to go through two traffic circles (Traffic circles are a Washington D.C. trademark.) Traffic enters into these circles from all directions, with very few drivers looking to yield to on-coming cars. It can be a dizzying experience. On those occasions, where Dad had not gotten the tie quite right, he would re-work his knot as we navigated the circle with a hand or a knee. The first few times I experienced the "drive and dress" routine, it was a completely terrifying experience. Soon, it became part of the normal commute to Temple. In fact, I am hard pressed to remember any drive to Temple with my Dad (and there were hundreds) that did not require some type of dress and drive.

By the time we arrived, he was in full Rabbi attire and no one could have guessed he had just left the house twenty minutes ago, half naked. I have taught all three of my children how to drive. I love to tell all my kids stories about their Papa Joe. However, this is one I never shared.

The Temple commute could always be eventful. One drive on Rosh Hashanah eve was particularly memorable. As I mentioned in a previous chapter, our synagogue, given the size our congregation, would hold two services in the evening of the high holidays – an early service at 6:00 p.m. and the second service that followed at 8:45 p.m. In order to have holiday dinner, we would actually have to start holiday dinner at our house around 3:30 p.m. so that by 5:00, 5:15, we could get down to Temple. You could not be late or cut it close at the High Holidays.

We typically had family and a few friends over for holiday dinner (really much closer to lunch). This particular year, we had our newest rabbi, Rabbi

Bruce Lustig, over for our holiday meal (or pre-game meal, as I thought about it, being a sports fan.) Rabbi Lustig was fresh from rabbinic school and ready to experience his first High Holidays at WHC. We finished our dinner and saw it was a few minutes after 5:00; it was time to get going. Dad, Rabbi Lusting, and I all left in Dad's car with the others to follow with mom. I do remember Dad was already fully dressed, so no "knee driving" necessary for this trip. I could see Rabbi Lustig was already a little nervous. Who could blame him? As I said in a previous chapter, the high holidays are the Super Bowl for a rabbi, and it was his first go around. Even dad, a veteran, was always nervous during the holidays.

Off we went in Dad's red Honda Prelude. There are a few different routes to take to Temple and this day, in order to avoid traffic, dad thought we would jump on the highway to cut off some of the local traffic. We headed up Democracy Avenue to the entrance ramp of the freeway. We began looping our way into the merging lanes when all of the sudden, we saw it, complete gridlock. The highway was a parking lot. Cars bumper to bumper, brake lights on, and everything at a complete standstill. This presented a big problem. The start time for services ("kick-off time") was fast approaching. Rabbi Lustig looked concerned. I was concerned. What to do? Dad, he had no concerns. He simply flipped the car into reverse and proceeded to back-up. You read correctly, he *backed-up* the highway entrance ramp. He backed up not just ten or fifteen feet, he backed up the entire length of the entrance ramp. We were almost down the entire length of the ramp, it was not a matter of backing-up a few feet, it was probably at least 100 yards! If Rabbi Lustig was not anxious at the start of our journey, now, half-way up the entrance ramp in reverse, the sweat was clearly evident on his forehead. We made it all the way up the ramp, not without a few puzzled/angry drivers, and few who didn't know as they honked they had just flipped off the rabbi on the most holy of days. Eventually, we made it to the WHC parking lot, in time and ready for services. Just another commute with Dad to his place of work.

Dad and his adventurous driving stories, are not just limited to commutes to Temple. Growing up, mom and dad took us on fantastic vacations to Europe. Most trips, we rented a car so we could drive from country to country. As mom and dad were fond of saying,

"Kids, this is how you are really able to see and experience the country."

Dad was the sole driver for all of these trips. He managed to navigate the streets and highways of Europe well, except for England. Every time we made a right or left turn in London, I had the fear of god put in me, as we always ended up on the wrong side of the road.

During one of our trips to Europe, we got lost in the middle of an Italian town. Mom and dad were struggling with directions. They are argued back and forth. Mom insisted we ask for directions. Dad, like most men, wasn't having any of it. Finally, he broke down, and rolled down his window to ask for help. Instead of merely asking the question in plain old English, Dad thought if he spoke broken English with an Italian accent, somehow the old Italian villager would better understand him. Instead, the man gave us a blank stare. We continued along, still lost, when all of the sudden…

"Joe, you are in the piazza!" Mom screamed. Sure enough, somehow, dad had gotten our car in the middle of an Italian piazza – fountain , cafes, and all. An entire town of Italians sipping their expresso, looking in wonderment as to how this American could have gotten his car and family in the middle of the square.

"Oh my god, oh my god," Mom continued (she has a flair for the dramatic).

"Children get down, get down" she hollered as she herself crouched on the floor of the passenger side. Rachel, Josh, and I were half embarrassed, half in hysterics at where we ended up.

Dad, cool as ever, responded, "Oh Marcia, take it easy, relax, kids look at that beautiful fountain."

We eventually made it out and back to the road. Mom and Dad were right, in this case, renting a car really allowed us to see and experience a country. Real up close and real personal.

For all of dad's interesting driving habits and experiences, he was a great driver when it came to our Weinberg day-trips to the beach.

Given a Rabbi's hectic schedule, it was not often we could get away as a family for an entire weekend. However on certain Sundays during the summer, when the schedule allowed, dad would pile us in the car and head to the Delaware shore for a day at the beach. He would wake us up at 5:45 a.m. so by 6:00, we would be in the car. He would tell us, "close your eyes, go back to sleep."

He then would drive two and half to three hours to the Delaware shore. At 9:00 a.m. he would excitedly call out, "Kids we are here, its breakfast time."

That began a great beach day for the Weinberg Five. Jumping the waves, taking long walks, and of course, the traditional Weinberg end of day, highly intense game of scrabble, were all part of our beach day routine. Dad always insisted we stayed on the beach as long as possible, not wanting the day to end. It would usually be close to 7:00 before he agreed it was time to pack-up. We headed to the public showers (that is not a place I look back on with fond memories,) showered, and got dressed. Dinner was always at the Rusty Rudder in Dewey Beach, Delaware, our dining spot for so many years. We would finish dinner around 9:00 – 9:30, make a quick trip to the Rehoboth Boardwalk for some ice cream and Candy Kitchen fudge, and then at 10:00 p.m. it was time to pile back into the car and head home. Dad would load us back in the car, often times with a painful sunburn.

"Guys, put your head down and go to sleep," he would say. Two and half or three hours later, close to 1:00 a.m., we would be back home.

"We are home, run up to your room and get in bed." For dad, this was a 19 hour day, with close to 6 hours of driving. He never complained. He never seemed tired. He was just happy we were all together and had a great day at the beach. Those days, dad was not only a top notch driver, he was a first- rate navigator, steering our family in a wonderful and happy direction.

What person most influenced your father's Rabbinate?

As I mentioned earlier, many PK questions are questions people had for their Rabbi. Many congregants, and lots of my friends, were curious how my father ended up becoming a Rabbi, what led him down that path, and who or what experiences influenced him.

Many Rabbis come from a long line of rabbi's dating back hundreds of years in their family. However, this was not the case, as my dad did not come from a long line of rabbis. In fact, there were no rabbis in his family. He did have an Uncle Leopold who was a Cantor in Germany, but there were no other rabbis or cantors in his family.

I do think Dad's early childhood played a major part in shaping the person he became and his choice to become a rabbi.

Dad tells the story in a 1997 sermon:

> *It was a bitter cold Chicago January in 1939. My father, who had been gone many days, stood framed in the doorway of our apartment, behind him, the shadowy figures of an old man and woman, my Opa and Oma (the German name for Grandpa and Grandma).*
>
> *This was just two months after the infamous Kristallnaht, when the organized Nazi hate campaign against Jews exploded. Hundreds of synagogues and Jewish-owned businesses were destroyed. In every city and town, Jews were arrested. Some, like my Opa, were taken for brutal interrogation at police stations, others to concentration camps.*
>
> *Hearing this horrible news, my father, who had emigrated to the United States years earlier, made the dangerous journey back to Germany to rescue this parents and other relatives.*
>
> *They came to live in our home. I was just a toddler. My Oma died soon after, and for the next seven years, my Opa and I shared the same*

bedroom. He took me on wonderful walks to Lincoln Park along Lake Michigan. On the coldest days, I would climb inside his huge overcoat. And on Shabbat, sitting next to his tallit-draped figure, he taught me the prayers and when to say "Ohmain."

I believe the wonderful and close friendship Dad shared with his grandfather, rescued from Nazi Germany, and the courageous actions of his father (my grandfather) had an indelible imprint on my father. Dad did not have to read about the Holocaust in a textbook and how it almost extinguished the Jewish people, it was real life. It was his grandpa pulled out of Nazi Germany with almost no time to spare. It was the real life example of his father risking everything going back to Germany to pull his family out of harm's way. Dad saw firsthand what it means to never sit and be a bystander. Instead, no matter the consequences or the circumstances, to be called to action and to stand-up and make a difference.

Once Dad become a Rabbi, there is no doubt the one person and experience that shaped him for years to come.

Central to Dad's rabbinate was the idea of standing up for what you believe in. He would always preach to his congregation not be silent, to stand and be counted. I think this idea was born out of dad's experience in marching with Martin Luther King Jr. in 1965. That moment and that man, I believe, had the greatest impact of my father and fashioned the type of rabbi he would become.

Dad was ordained as a rabbi in the spring of 1963 as the struggle for civil rights took center stage in this country. Right out of rabbinic school, Dad took a job at his first congregation, Temple Emanuel in San Francisco. Two years later, in March of 1965, on the heels of "Bloody Sunday" in Selma, Alabama, the call went out to clergy across the country to come to Selma and march with Dr. King. A group of Bay Area Rabbis, including dad, answered the call. He had just turned twenty-eight. He left behind his wife and his two year old daughter and was bound for Alabama. While there was real danger and real fear given the events taking place, Dad felt it was his calling. He believed he needed to stand with Dr. King and be counted.

The experience and its impact never left my father, and he wrote about it in an essay entitled "Purim in Selma" (The march coincided with the Jewish holiday of Purim.) The following is an expert of his writing:

> *Sunday morning, the day of the beginning of the great march, people began to congregate in front of Browns Chapel as early as nine o'clock. By ten o'clock, many thousands had gathered. Mighty throngs joined together in the singing of freedom songs and religious hymns. Finally, late in the morning the religious service began. Rabbi Abraham Heschel read the scriptural portion from the Old Testament. Following this Reverend Ralph Abernathy came forward to the platform to introduce Dr. Martin Luther King. When King entered and made his way through the thousands that had gathered, he was mobbed and almost crushed by the throng. Everyone stretched out their hand trying desperately to greet this great and dedicated leader. In his introduction, Reverend Abernathy placed him in a line of great emancipators, from Abraham through Moses and Joshua. Indeed, I felt as I listed to Dr. King's words, standing on the steps of Browns Chapel that memorable Sunday morning that he had not exaggerated the role of this man. He spoke with simplicity and yet with great eloquence. He spoke gently with love and compassion even for those who were his enemies and yet his voice carried with it a strength of unswerving determination that gave all who heard him the confidence that our cause would surely be won.*
>
> *After the conclusion of his speech, somehow miraculously, the thousands who had gathered formed themselves into a gigantic procession, eight abreast, and followed Dr. King, Ralph Bunche and a host of others down the dirt road called Sylvan Street in the main business section of Selma. There, as we passed through the center of town, groups of white people gathered at each corner in front of stores, seeking to intimidate the marchers. But in all cases, it proved in vain.*
>
> *We marched out of the town and up the hill leading to the Edmond Pettus Bridge crossing the Alabama River, where only two weeks earlier, Alabama State troopers became storm troopers and cruelly attacked the*

a similar line of marchers. Now, the great throng of almost 8,000 from every section of the country, even from the far state of Hawaii, of every color, of every creed, marched hand in hand.

As I looked up at the sea of people stretched out before me crossing the bridge, I could not help think of the words of the Passover Haggadah, "And we shall remembers that we were slaves unto Pharaoh in the Land of Egypt and the Lord they God took thee out from thence with a strong hand and an outstretched arm and when thy children ask in times to come what does this mean, thou shall say, this is because of the Lord did for me when I was a slave in Egypt."

And so I marched that warm Sunday afternoon down a highway in Alabama, arm in arm with an Asian, Christian, Jew, and Buddhist. All of us were marching to testify that in our generation we too would participate in the redemption of our brethren from the land of Egypt.

Rabbi, are we going to win today?

Every rule has an exception and so this book and the list of questions have one exception. Clearly, this was not a PK question. Instead this is a straight-up R (Rabbi) question. I was present when it was asked. I include it in this book because I think it provides some additional insight into the life of a rabbi (and his family) when outside the Temple.

The question was not asked in a tongue and cheek manner, or with a wide grin. It was not asked in a manner a friend might ask another friend.

"How do you think we will play today," or "do you think our team is up to the challenge?"

No, this question was asked in a serious, straight-up manner.

Dad and I were taking our seats at RFK Stadium minutes before kick-off. As we searched for our row and seat number, Dad was spotted by a congregant sitting a few rows away.

"Rabbi, Rabbi," he called out. "Are we going to win today?"

The questioner was all business, he wanted to know what Dad knew, meaning, "you're a man of God and have an "in," so let me in on the final score. Honest, this man was not kidding. The congregant asked the question as if judgment day, rather than kick-off, was upon us.

Dad could see the seriousness of the question and the questioner, but tried to play it off with a laugh or two, but our congregant was not having any laughs. At this point, I suppose Dad could have launched into a response, stating that just because he is a Rabbi does not give him the inside into the outcomes of sporting events. (That would have a nice gig if it did, I would have liked to find a local bookie if that were the case.) With kick-off approaching, Dad gave the smart answer,

"I'm afraid not," he said.

Why smart? If the Redskins, won the congregant would be so happy with the win he would probably forget dad had gotten it wrong. If, however, the Redskins lost (and they often did growing up,) then dad was right on the mark. His connection or "direct line" to the man upstairs was intact and maybe the congregant would up his pledge to the Temple, given the rabbi and his closeness with God.

Does your Dad ever get a day off?

Growing up, it was hard for me to relate or compare my dad's profession to my friends' parents and their various jobs. They found it strange my dad was not home most nights for dinner. I found it part of the territory. I could, in some ways, relate to kids whose parents were doctors, for a rabbi is much like a surgeon on call. When a patient needs immediate medical attention, morning, noon, or night, the surgeon is always on call. If someone needed help, it is the doctor's job to be at the ready. So it was for dad and congregants in need. (Before cell phones, dad actually wore a beeper just like a surgeon so he could be reachable at any time.)

As a rabbi to over 3,000 families and close to 10,000 people, dad was never "off duty". He had very few days off. To be clear, dad never complained or bemoaned the fact he was on-call twenty-four/seven. He loved what he did, he viewed it as his calling, and from that standpoint, running to the hospital late at night or jumping up from the dinner table to be with a family who was in need, that was part and parcel of the profession.

Growing up in Montgomery County Maryland we loved when it snowed, for that meant no school. Our county was famous (and still is) for canceling school if they see a flake or two. We loved our snow days. For dad, there was never such a thing as a snow day. While my siblings and I might stay in our pajamas for an entire snow day, Dad eventually needed to make the wardrobe change from pjs to black suit.

Jennifer Cornfield, a woman in our congregation, wrote our family about dad and the snow day of all snow days:

> *"My Bat Mitzvah occurred at the time of what was then called "The Blizzard of the Century" in March of 1993. It wasn't typical to be stuck in a hotel, totally immobilized thanks to snow that measured in*

feet rather than inches. What was incredible to me and my family was the sight of Rabbi Weinberg as he walked through the door of the Marriott Suites Hotel in Bethesda. There he was, in a winter coat and boots covered with snow, carrying the precious Torah. He did this so that two young men and I could become B'nai Mitzvah as planned before an assemblage of over one hundred stranded members of our out of town families. On the most special day for me and my family, I learned how extraordinary this man is and to what lengths he will go to express his commitment to this congregational family."

A day off? Not Joe Weinberg, that was not in his DNA. There was too much to do and too many to care of to take a day off.

What is the best sermon your dad ever gave?

This is a hard question. It is kind of like asking the son whose dad manages a Baskin-Robbins what is your favorite flavor ice cream. There are many special words, messages, and sermons he delivered to his congregation over the thirty years of his rabbinate. Trying to pick one is a daunting task. While the question used the term "best" in answering it I am drawn to most meaningful. I am fortunate to have many of his sermons and have read through most of them. After much research, there are two (actually one and a half) I will share.

The first is from Yom Kippur 1985, a sermon on teen suicide. Dad loved Rachel, Josh, and me, his children, and he also loved the children of Washington Hebrew Congregation. He would frequently show up at the Temple's Early Childhood Center (now named the Rabbi Joseph Weinberg Early Childhood Center) and get down on his hands and knees to play and laugh with the three and four year-olds. Dad also looked forward to attending weekend religious school retreats with the 8th and 9th grade students. By spending the weekend together at camp, Dad felt he started to connect with each of them and began to form relationships and friendships. It was one of his favorite activities at the Temple. He also had a passion for teaching kids; he was so full of energy and enthusiasm when talking to young people.

As I was finishing up the first draft of this book, I ran into a congregant having coffee with two other women. She introduced me, "this is Rabbi Weinberg's son." She then continued to tell the ladies about her favorite Rabbi Weinberg story.

"I will never forget when Scott was in Confirmation Class, Rabbi Weinberg was speaking to the kids about the dangers of drinking and driving. The Rabbi actually gave out his home phone number to the entire class that night and told the kids if they ever needed a ride that they should call him. The two women seemed amazed. For dad, that was embedded into his character, and he cared deeply about all his congregants and, chief among them, the kids of the Temple. It was this love and the terrible plight of teen suicide that made this (and still today make this) a powerful and important message.

L'Chayim: To The Life of Our Children
Yom Kippur
September 25, 1985

"Yitgadal v'yitkadash, Shme Rabbah" - the words of Kaddish familiar to every Jew – Words of Loss- of separation- of farewell. Words of comfort in times of despair- or even strength in moments of uncertain trembling.

At this season of Remembrance at the Yizkor Memorial Service – this afternoon we will say Kaddish for the generation that has gone. This morning, we say it for another generation. America's children who are destroying their lives in larger and larger numbers.

From last Yom Kippur to this day, more than 6,000 of our teenagers committed suicide, an increase of 300% in the last two decades and this is only a small portion of a massive collage—pain, death, and destruction.

Suicide is now the second leading cause of death among teenagers after accidents- and we know that many accidents are, in reality, unrecorded suicides.

What else is in the mind of a youth who gets himself blind drunk and then guns the family car down River Road or the Beltway?

In addition to teenage suicides, that succeed, 25,000 a year try – but don't quite make it to the Kaddish list. It is estimated adolescent suicide attempts have tripled every year. It is a frightening epidemic which touches more and more of America's families and neighborhoods and shakes us to the very depths of our being.

Nationwide alarm and concern has led to an avalanche of feature articles, television specials, Teen Hotlines, Crisis Centers, and, just three months ago, a National Conference on Teen Suicide as a culmination of President Reagan's Youth Suicide Prevention Month.

The Union of America Hebrew Congregations, the parent body of American Reform Judaism, has established Yad Ha-Tikvah a task force on suicide concerns and here in the nation's capital, there is now a National Center for the Prevention of Youth Suicide.

However, we are not talking of conferences, statistics, or percentages here. We are speaking of human life. We are not speaking of older adults, or the critically or incurably ill. We are talking about children, 12, 14, and 17-year-old kids, with, so it seems, everything going for them – bright futures, the popular admired kid on the team or in the school play, the youngster who seemed to have it all together.

And then, one day – like a thunderbolt – he explodes. He opts out; says "no" to life. "I want to die so I won't hurt anymore!"

Sixteen-year-old Craig put a hose to his car's exhaust pipe. He left a note expressing his love for his family and asking their forgiveness because he "could never live up to their expectations."

Fifteen-year- old Perry ran away from home often, got into trouble with the police, drank a lot, and skipped classes. He was angry, and everyone seemed to be angry at him. He shot himself soon after having been confronted with stealing money from his parents.

Marissa was a nineteen-year-old college freshman. She began to skip meals, became lethargic, withdrawn, and fatigued. She couldn't concentrate on study and became obsessed with death. In art class, she painted a young woman sprawled on a bathroom floor, pills scattered about. She titled her canvas, Marissa-cide.

This is the carnage of young people who have given up, for whom things have become so bad, for whom the hassles of life have no answer but death.

Young suicide – the extreme, explosive giving up on life – tells us something unhealthy, undesirable, dangerous, even treacherous is going on in that secret "far country" – that world of youth culture

Fenced with the warning, "No trespassing!"

"Adults keep out!"

The statistics – the data – of death and destruction, of despair and pain, the stories of young life and tragic premature death, do not, of course, suggest this is happening to all our youth.

However, there are other things going on in the world of our teenagers – dangerous and threatening – to our children, and of deep concern to all of us parents and grandparents; responsible adults of society.

We are discovering, to our dismay, children are experimenting with life and death in frightening ways. Not only with drugs, alcohol, and combinations of the two, but procedures with their bodies, to achieve special highs, unusual pleasure or pain. These are not harmless games or fantasies.

These are life threatening and mind-boggling experiments. They are putting children at great risk of injury, crippling, temporary or permanent impairments, psychological damage, personality change, and, yes, death itself. Death! You know! This year has made us all know – death itself!

Our kids are trying these awful things and not telling. Or their friends are doing them and, in a twisted sense of loyalty, a perverse ethic which says, "Don't be a tattletale, a stool pigeon," they are not telling. Many are afraid to share, and carry the heavy burden of keeping these horrible secrets.

What's going on here? What's happening to our young? It has, we all know, never been easy to be a teenager. Developmentally, it is a traumatic time of life. The body is changing. The young boy or girl is in middle passage, no longer a child but not quite an adult. It is a time, as Goethe once described it, of "Sturn and Drang" – of turmoil and pressure, vast changes in metabolism, moods. At one instant, a pouting, natural child, the next, an adult, all grown up, yet with so much further to go.

It is that season of life when we reach the zenith of our physical energy, but are still limited in opportunity to give it expression and free rein. We are pulled in many directions – carefree play and serious responsibility, building for the future, yet yearning to celebrate ourselves and the moment. The world is at our feet. The future is ours.

But this is not the ebullient temper of the contemporary teenager. The mood of many of today's youth represents a radical departure from most previous generations. When the conversation in a discussion group, during a retreat, turned to the capture of the slasher in Los Angeles, I remarked, "thank goodness, he's been caught."

"Yeah," replied the kids. "But he's probably going to sell his story to the National Inquirer *for a million dollars."*

There is a perverse cynicism among the young people, manifested in a dark view of the world. They are not even sure the world will last. When I asked another group of students what they thought life would be like in the year 2000, their responses were all prefaced with "If we are not all blown up before then."

The mass culture (as well as the environment,) which surrounds our young, both reflects and feeds their mood and temperament; their cynicism and despair. It mirrors and shapes their perceptions and their tastes.

As of last year, I learned that "Prince" is not someone who lives in Windsor Castle, so this year I've discovered that "Madonna" is not part of Christian theology.

"We are living in a material world and I am a material girl... The guy with the cold hard cash is always Mister Right," coos Madonna.

Materialism is everything! Get it anyway you can!

The words, beat, and flashy videos, which accompany much of the contemporary pop music, reflect a pounding energy that all too often has no real purpose or direction. It is a violent and vile release of confusion, frustration, anger, and aggression.

"We're not going to take it anymore," sings Twisted Sister, *as the accompanying video flashes scenes of a rock loving son pushing his father out the window.*

Miami Vice *currently tops in TV ratings, and is one long, glitzy series of blood and brutality. In popular culture, sex is not portrayed as a loving, affectionate, warm relationship.*

"Sounds like an animal panting to the beat," sings rock star, Judas Priest.

Sex is crude and, most especially, manipulative. It is use and be used. There is no real intimacy; tenderness. A deep personal relationship requires risks. It means revealing and sharing the self. In doing so, we are subject to profound humiliation, rejection, and mockery! For many, the solution is, "don't get hurt, don't get emotionally involved..."

The costumes, the fashion and dress of today's youth, similarly reflects that same hard, tough, protective quality. Even the mannequins at the Hecht's Teen Department look like they need counseling. You try to avert your eyes from their icy stare.

It is as though Halloween has come early this year. The exaggerated make-up, hairstyles, and clothes mask the teenagers' true identity. No one will see the real me.

In addition to a mean and crude quality in pop-culture, and a dark view of the nuclear world, for increasing numbers of our young, the uncertain tempestuous adolescent years coincidentally have become a time of personal family upheaval.

As they embark, gingerly, on the unchartered stormy voyage of adolescence, needing every support, their parents arrive at mid-life, deciding it's time for a new life, city, career, playmate, a new marriage, a second family. "What new developments, bizarre series of events, await me this day, in the latest episode of As my family turns."

Too often, Mom and Dad are not at home. Frenetically, they pursue the agenda of their own "angst" – their mortality, their "hang-ups." But even when they are physically present, the head and the mind are pre-occupied. A troubled girl sits despondently in school detention, the movie The Breakfast Club. *Trying to break through, a friend asks "Your parents? So, what do they do to you?"*

There is a long pause, and then she answers, "They ignore me!"

Indifference, isolation, giving up on relationships, the plaintive longing, the desperate plea of our kids is also the theme song of the Breakfast Club, *"Don't you forget about me! Please don't forget about me."*

In addition to all the other influences, our children are also bludgeoned by another reality – the demands of a successful life; an itinerary for the road to success. Make the team. Get those A's. Bring home the top test score; AP classes, break the SAT scoreboard.

"If I get a "B" they look at me with disgust!"

Do everything and anything to make your resume look good. Popularity, a host of friends, acceptance by your peers, as well as the college of choice, the pressures from within and without beat down upon the young.

It was so very different for many of us. We couldn't fail to succeed. As children or grandchildren of immigrants, any college was an improvement. Better jobs were assured and so were bigger homes, higher salaries, and status.

Today, the pressures on the young are staggering. Many can't take it. They break out, cry out – escape, run, explode – weekend keg parties, the newest drug, the Beltway's fast lane.

"Yitgadel, viyitkadash, Shme Rabbah."

So what shall we do? How shall we break the vicious cycle? Reclaim, revive, restore our most precious gift – our beloved children?

This Yom Kippur day is a time of fasting, when we set aside "the material world." We turn to the spiritual, the more sustaining dimension of life. The fast of this day of reflection – the reordering of our priorities – is a model for us and our children. We have to turn from empty calories, gorging ourselves and our children on meaningless, plastic experiences and a nauseating buffet of material junk, to the real "soul food" of life.

To begin with, our children crave our love and affection, time and attention, even when they are not being affectionate or acting lovable. In addition, they must have wise counsel and helpful direction from adults whom they feel they can trust and turn to as a sounding board. Friends are wonderful, but children also need the perspective of an adult who has been there, who can say, "I know about depression. I've been depressed. Everyone has. It is part of life. But here are some things that were helpful to me."

You, who are older members of our Congregation, should know that many of our students often say how easy it is for them to talk to a grandparent or older adult. Here is an opportunity, more often than you may suspect, to enhance and even save life. The neighborhood and community should be part of a support system, as well. There was a time, years ago, when no child could walk down the street without every neighbor knowing it. I'm not suggesting everyone become a Yenta. But we do have to help each other. We cannot wall ourselves off in our own home and say, "it's none of our business." If we see a serious problem, it is "our business!"

Let me also plead with you, the youngster members of our Temple, to understand the true meaning of friendship. If you know someone is doing something risky, unhealthy, or dangerous, if they are in deep trouble, if they are beginning to act in strange ways – eating, drinking, sleeping too much or too little – then you have got to tell; sound the alarm. Don't think, "Oh, I'm probably exaggerating!" you don't want to be sorry later. Tell some responsible adult. It's not up to you to solve the problem, but you know! You may be the only one!

We, at Washington Hebrew Congregation, are aware of this need for our kids to talk, to share, to build relationships. This is one of the main goals of our Camp WHC Retreat Weekends. In addition, as part of our Youth Program, we hope shortly to establish a Teen Hotline – a phone number – available to our young people whenever they have the need. Another vital ingredient in a healthy spiritual diet for our kids is "self-esteem." In our effort to give and do everything for our young, we sometimes rob them of wonderful, self-affirming experiences, hard and meaningful work.

How instructive, in this regard, was the Live Aid Concert of this summer. Young people around the world pooled their enthusiasm, energy, talent, and resources to participate in and produce an unprecedented media event. Reaching out to help the starving millions, they were uplifted and inspired, in the process. They discovered the joy of purposeful giving. They found that life is not "a meaning." It is an opportunity for meaningful experiences.

This is the same lesson so many of our 10th graders learn each year when they do Social Service Confirmation Projects. Visiting the hospitals and nursing homes, or teaching skills to the handicapped and the retarded, the blind or the deaf, they receive, as they give, the reward of self-esteem and fulfillment. In this way, they become more hopeful, optimistic people.

The Bible tells the story of the prophet, Jeremiah, and the destruction of Jerusalem by the Babylonians. As the city is besieged, the great prophet hears the battering rams of the victorious conquerors destroying the gates, the last defenses of his beloved city. At this moment, the moment of his deepest despair, God speaks to Jeremiah and commands, "purchase a homestead – buy a portion of the land."

Perform a symbolic act of faith. In the midst of the darkest hour of defeat, you declare hope. You, in word and act, say, there will yet come a better day.

It is that mood of hopefulness – of optimism – of enthusiasm for life we must re-kindle in our young. The zest to climb every mountain, wrestle every obstacle, tame the wilderness, has defined youth.

It is that joyous affirmation which is echoed in the exuberant chords of the popular Israeli folk song, written for the soldier who yearns so desperately for life, Od Lo Ahavti Dai.

"I've done much in my lifetime, but there is still so much more to do. I've built many houses, but not yet the house of my dreams. I have planted vineyards, but not all the hills I can reach. I haven't painted a flower or discovered how the road will lead me or whither I go. I haven't yet done everything with my very own hands. I haven't written my memoirs yet or finished composing the song of my life."

Write. Write passages of love and hope.

And compose. Compose a song.

That sings the beauty and the pulse beat of every glorious tomorrow.

Amen.

The "half" of a sermon is from the Yom Kippur Yiskor service in 1997. Yiskor, the Hebrew word for "memory," is a special service held during Yom Kippur day where Jews remember those loved ones who have died. However, dad's message in this sermon was not about death, rather it was all about life. It is a story personal to our family, but one that carries with it an important lesson. He said:

Death teaches us yet another lesson. Not only to treasure the time we have with our loved ones, but that our answer to death must be more life. This became my own most profound, personal understanding this past year.

Last Yom Kippur our family's heart was filled with a single prayer,

"Dear God, please let our treasured Elaine, sister, sister-in-law, wife, mother, aunt – be healed."

For thirteen months, from the day of her diagnosis, Elaine battled. From chemotherapy in the morning to the lecture platform that afternoon, from the hospital one day to the seminar leader the next. But when in June, it was clear that she was so rapidly slipping away from us, her son Jeremy who had just become engaged, resolved,

"My mom must know that our family is going forward. Mom cannot die without knowing that Shira and I are married."

In twenty-four hours we put together a wedding. Flowers, corsages, yes even champagne from the Golan Heights where Jeremy had proposed to his future bride. Our children brought the Chuppah from Washington, Shira's family including grandparents, flew to Chicago from Birmingham and her grandma's wedding dress was miraculously a perfect fit. We found a Klezmer band, invited the closest of relatives, and turned the lounge next to Elaine's room at Highland Park Hospital into a wedding chapel.

Elaine's last moment of consciousness was seeing Jeremy in his tuxedo and Shira in her satin wedding gown.

Afterward, we came back to the house with the Klezmers playing quietly in the background. And, then, almost inexplicitly as the Klezmers broke into the strains of Hava Negilah, we found ourselves in a circle in the garden surrounded by the flowers that Elaine had planted that spring. Hands reaching for each other, arms locked in a single embrace and our feet moving rhymically through the grass. Round and round we went, encircling the bride and groom, smiling, even laughing.

At that moment, we didn't understand ourselves what was happening. But later, we realized, we were saying, "Death, you will not have the final victory!"

It was a moment of the most amazing affirmation of life.

Later that afternoon, we all returned to the hospital. Jeremy and Shira, bride and groom, curled up next to Elaine, spending their first night and Elaine's last holding her hand in theirs.

We grieved, but because of our moment in the garden at Jeremy and Shira's wedding, we understand that even as everything around us shouts, "No" we must again and again say "Yes" to life!

How many times have you been to Israel?

The question makes sense, much like a logical math problem. Your dad is a rabbi, plus Israel is a big part of the Jewish faith and religion, equals, you must have traveled to Israel a lot. In my case, the equation adds up. Growing up as a preacher's kid, I was fortunate enough to visit the Land of Israel many times.

When I was eight years old, Dad started the tradition of summer family congregational trips to Israel. These were amazing experiences. Each trip usually consisted of approximately fifty people (enough to fill one tour bus.) Our group had people of all ages, but was mostly comprised of families. For three weeks, all of these separate families quickly merged into one large family as our tour bus zigzagged up and down the Land of Israel. I went on six of these trips growing up, and a seventh after Jennifer and I were married, taking her to Israel for the first time. While each of these visits had a similar itinerary, and many of the same stops, and I knew the stories as well as some of our tour guides, the trips never became old. While the tour stop might be the same, the group changed. There were new families and new kids to hang with. Each time I visited Israel, I was a little older and began to better appreciate the country and its people. I also think Israel – the places and the stories – never get old or stale, no matter how many times you have visited.

Each trip had a similar dynamic. Mom and Dad were the trip leaders. They were responsible for everyone; for the entire group.

"Is everyone on the bus?"

"Did everyone get on the plane?"

"Is everyone set for dinner tonight?"

"Does everyone have enough water?"

This meant that our nuclear family, the Weinberg family, would need to take a back seat from time to time to make sure the group was taken care of. For the most part, Rachel, Josh, and I got it and went with the flow. From time to time, it could be a little frustrating, like getting to a rest stop in the middle of a 90 degree day, and not be able to find your mom or dad to get a few shekels so you could buy a coke because they were behind the building making sure everyone found the restrooms. But playing second fiddle was part of the gig of being a PK on these trips. It was part of the territory, not a big deal...Except on one or two occasions.

It was our second family trip and I was nine years old. Please remember this important fact as you read the story. We were on our tour bus headed to Jerusalem when our tour guide, Yaakov, informed us we were all in for a special treat.

"The hotel you would be staying at for the next six nights is The Plaza, Israel's newest, most modern hotel, and, kids," he said in this thick Israeli accent. "You are going to love the swimming pool."

This news had the group upbeat and excited. We certainly did not stay in dumps or run-down establishments during our trips, however, our hotels were, from time to time, a little spartan, after all, this was Israel in the mid-seventies. We had just spent two nights at a kibbutz in Northern Israel. While being on a kibbutz was a fantastic experience, it was far from the Ritz. We pulled up and Yaakov had not lied. The Plaza was big, beautiful, and modern. Mom and Dad went directly to the front desk to collect all the keys. This was the drill at every hotel. While everyone else started to unload the bags from the bus, they checked in and got each families' room assignment. At the front desk, there was commotion, Dad, Yaakov, the man behind the desk, now two or three additional hotel employees, papers, phone calls, I could not tell what was going. There seemed to be lots of commotion, hands waving and finger pointing. I thought it was just the typical Israeli theatrics. We located our bags and pulled them to the side. We waited while mom and dad passed out all the keys to the families. After they all cleared out and headed to their rooms, Rachel inquired,

"Mom what is our room number?"

"Kids," mom started out in that voice. You know, that voice; the voice that immediately signals you're not going to like what I am about to say, but try to understand. That voice. "There was a mix-up with the hotel reservations and they were missing one of the family's rooms."

"Too bad for them," I said. "What is our room number? I want to hit the pool"

"We are staying at a different hotel up the street," Mom said. "We can't have a family staying in another hotel while we stay here."

Dad came over to begin a sermon about our family's responsibility to the others on the trip, but we were not in the mood for a sermon on "PK responsibility." The three Weinberg kids launched into full protest,

Why us? To be here in the lobby of the Plaza, to see the wonderful pool, the injustice of it all (I told you, you had to read this story remembering I was only nine years old at the time). Mom continued in that voice, that voice that tells you what I am about to tell you is a load of crap.

"We are going to a lovely hotel called The Kings, and it's just up the street."

As we gathered our bags and headed up the street to The Kings, I saw my friends in their bathing suits passing by the lobby, heading to the pool.

"Where are you going?" they yelled out.

I decided rather than launch into a tirade about the sacrifices we PKs must make, I would ignore it and head up the road. Let me tell you, The Kings was no Plaza; not even close.

On another congregational trip, we flew from New York to London, switched plans at Heathrow Airport, and then flew on to Israel. I did not sleep at all on the flight to London. It was exciting to be on a plane overnight, and I was too busy talking to my new friends. We got to the departure lounge for our flight to Tel Aviv. It was packed with people, bodies crammed into almost every chair and all over the floor. They announced there would be a slight delay in boarding. Unable to keep my eyes open, I was able to find an empty chair and fell dead asleep.

The next thing I know, I awoke feeling refreshed. There was just one tiny issue. The entire lounge was completely empty. Not a soul, not a bag, nothing but a completely empty departure lounge. Before I could fully comprehend what was going on, I see my dad running up the ramp from the airplane, pushing open the door to the gate with a half-smile and half sheepish look on his face.

"OK, Jono, time to get on the plane." He grabbed my hand and we boarded what was a completely full flight to a mix of some laughs, some stares, and some looks of disgust.

I had fallen asleep, and about 20 minutes later, they started boarding the flight. Mom and Dad went into familiar "leader mode," making sure everyone was onboard.

"The Ackermans? Check. The Shermans? Check. The elderly couple? Check. They are all on the plane. Everyone accounted for, we are ready to head to the Land of Israel. All on board except for… Me! Pre-occupied with getting the group on the plane, mom and dad missed just one who had not boarded the aircraft. Their son, Jonathan. I was still sound asleep in the lounge as the plane door was ready to close. It was a scene from Home Alone almost come to life.

Our Israel summer trips also taught me and my siblings to fend for ourselves.

In 1980, after Israel and Egypt signed their historic peace treaty, our congregational trip scheduled a stopover in Egypt on our way back from Israel. At the time, there were no direct flights from Tel Aviv to Cairo, so we boarded a bus and drove from Israel to Amman Jordan for a flight to Cairo on Royal Jordanian Airways. There was nothing royal about this airline. To this day, I swear someone brought a goat on-board the plane. On Israel trips, when it came to bag claim, be it at airports or hotels, we, the Weinberg kids, knew the drill. We had to get our family's bags as mom and dad would be tending to the rest of the group and helping those who needed a hand. Pretty simple job, and we were pros at it given this was our third family trip. However, the baggage claim at Cairo International Airport was like no place I had ever seen. It was a complete zoo; complete bedlam. I had never in my life seen a sea of humanity like this crammed into such a small place. I was twelve years old, and not a large kid for twelve. Josh, Rachel, and I made our way over to the baggage belt. This place was crazy. Our plan was for me to get to the belt and pass the bags back to Josh and Rachel. I pushed my way through people, over legs, under arms (someone needed to open up a deodorant stand in this place.) The noise was intense. Lots of Arabic screaming and shouting; commotion and chaos. There was a lot of pushing of bodies back and forth and I was getting swallowed up by this mass of Arabic humanity. The bags from our plane began to appear on the belt. All of a sudden, as someone pulled their bag off the belt, I lost my balance and got pushed on to the bag carrousel. No one seemed to care that a twelve year-old, small American boy with glasses was circling the belt with all the bags. I tried to get off the belt, but waves of people lining the belt made it impossible for me to get off. I tried to yell over to Josh and Rachel to no avail. The noise in the place was too loud, and so there I was, a Jewish American boy among the bags from Royal Jordanian Airways on a Cairo Egypt airport baggage carrousel.

After a trip around the carousal Dad spotted me on the belt, "Jono, will you please quit clowning around and be helpful, please?"

Our journeys to Israel also provided so many special moments. They became a staple of summer time growing up in our house. They provided a foundation for me, who I was as a person, what does it mean to be Jewish, and the importance of the support and defense of Israel. Among many special moments during those trips, there is one that stands out. It is a scene that, to this day, stays with me, and I use as a guide on how to live my life.

It was the summer of 1982, during this summer, Israel was involved in a military effort to stop rocket attacks that were being launched into Northern Israel from Lebanon. Waves of Israeli troops streamed into Lebanon to try to root out the terrorists who were conducting continual rocket attacks on the towns in northern Israel. The tour bus brought our group to a place called Rosh Hanikra on the Mediterranean seacoast. Rosh Hanikra is right on the boarder of Israel and Lebanon. Rosh Hanikra's main attraction is the beautiful limestone rock grottos. The way in which the beautiful blue water of the Mediterranean carved formations in and out of the rocks is an incredible sight. But for this visit, that scenery took a back-seat for me. During this summer, Rosh Hanikra served as a type of staging ground for Israeli troops as they prepared to head into Lebanon. This was the last stop before they headed into harm's way and into battle. I was fixated on the buses filled with 18 and 19 year-old Israeli boys. These were kids who were getting ready to head into Lebanon and into war. I starred at their faces. While I was a few years younger, they seemed like me. Like I was looking at the faces of me and my friends. I stood frozen as guilt began to overtake me.

How was this fair or right? Why do they have to fight? Why will some have to die while I will be getting on my air conditioned tour bus in the next few minutes and head for the next tour stop? They stuck their heads out the window and waved to us as the buses pulled out and disappeared over the border. The images, the faces, stayed with me for a long time. I had a difficult time for the rest of that trip, struggling with the question, "Why am I not on those buses? Why am I not doing my part?"

I thought for a long time that, upon turning 18, I must come to Israel, join the army, and fight. Ultimately, that is not the path I chose, and it is not without guilt from time-to-time that I did not pursue that direction. To this day, years later, I can still clearly make their faces out and I still feel, from time-to-time, that I took the easy way out. Whenever I hear of the death of an Israeli soldier, my mind flashes back to the faces leaning out of the window on the bus.

I think that day changed me. I did commit that I would not stand by the side of the road and watch the buses. I would be involved, no matter the issue of the cause, that experience, those faces speak to me today. Do not stand and watch, be involved. Make a difference.

One last family Israel trip story that is special to me:

On our third trip to Israel, we arrived in Jerusalem in the late afternoon. Our tradition on all of our trips was for the group to head to the Western Wall that night for our first visit to this most special and holy site in Jewish tradition. At night, the Wall is illuminated by light. The lights bathe the ancient stones, causing the wall to take on a golden color. It makes for a beautiful and powerful experience. At night in Jerusalem, the air is cool. The Wall is quiet and serene, there no large crowds, no tour guides, just a few people, some Hasidim dressed in all black rocking back and forth as they quietly prayed, and some tourists, like us. We stood in awe, some recited prayers, some touched the smooth stones that have stood for thousands of years, and other wrote hopes and prayers on tiny pieces of paper they fit into the cracks of the Wall. Like my two previous visits to the Wall, I went with my dad and brother and approached the Wall (Men and woman are separated at this place and must pray separately consistent with Orthodox tradition.) My dad whispered a few prayers as I closed my eyes and reached out to touch the Wall. All of sudden, tears began to well up within me. Try as I might to hold them back, I could not and I began to cry.

Dad did not turn to me and say, "What's wrong? Is everything OK?"

Instead, he quietly put his arm around me and pulled me closer. We kept our eyes closed and our heads resting on the wall. We spent a few more minutes together reciting prayers, and then headed to the bus and back to the hotel.

That night, as our parents tucked us into bed in our room, dad came over to me kissed me on the head and said, "That was special tonight."

It was. No questions, no inquiry, no sermons or discussion on my emotions. Just four words and a kiss goodnight. I am not sure how to explain my emotions that night. I had been to the Wall before, but I guess I had grown a little older and understood a little better what the place means to me, my people, and having my dad with me by my side at that moment. I think there are times in one's life that are so special, words or trying to express oneself do not do it justice. Instead, I think tears say all that needs to be said. I also reflect back on this moment not only for the time my dad and I shared, but also for the way in which a father interacted with his son. There were no big speeches or lots of questions, instead, he allowed the moment to happen, not interrupt it, but rather, to share in it and experience it. His small physical gesture, putting his arm around me, he told me all I needed to hear at that moment.

What was the best advice you received from your dad?

Even though he earned his living by being a preacher, surprisingly, dad was not one to give long speeches to his kids. I always felt mom was more the "speech giver" of the family. I think some of this had to do with the fact that giving advice and preaching sermons is what he did each and every day. At home it was time to turn that piece of him off. Dad was just happy to be home with us, to share a meal, to let us do the talking, and to hear what was on our minds.

Even though he did not do a lot of "sermonizing" when at home, my father instilled in me several important lessons. Live and celebrate every moment of every day. You cannot always control what challenges life presents, but how you face those circumstances, that is always in your control. And, make a difference, in the lives of one or many, make difference.

On the topic of celebrating life's big and small moments, I saved the card he sent me on my 18th birthday. I was a freshman at the University of Wisconsin-Madison by the time my 18th birthday rolled around, and his words struck a chord with me as I began my life away from home at college. I keep the card in my desk drawer at home and, from time to time, I still take it out to read. It provides me a guidepost on how to live my life.

> *Dear Mug:* (I am not sure why he called me that, I was usually Jono or sometimes Yoni, a shortened version of my Hebrew name, for some reason, he took to calling me "Mug" that year)
>
> *18! Unbelievable! But great! You have done so well these years and we are so proud of you !!!! We even miss you – occasionally. There is a very special quality of solid value and beautiful friendship which you reflect in everything you do and which make you such an esteemed person by peers and adults alike.*

Keep stretching, growing, reach for the best that is in you. There is so much good and potential there to bring you happiness and fulfillment. Celebrate your B Day, and make every day and your life a celebration.

Love,
Daaaaaaaaaad (that is the actual way the card is signed.)

I love that birthday card. I never get tired of reading it

Dad's other important piece of advice about how to deal with adversity or challenge was beautifully captured in a sermon he delivered shortly after Israel was attacked by Iraqi missiles, he said:

A simple drama on the stage of Jerusalem's concert hall, played for all the world to see, taught us the essence of human dignity and drama. The melodic strains of Isaac Stern's magical violin playing to an overflow audience were interrupted by the harsh wailing sirens, proclaiming a possible missile attack. The orchestra filed offstage, followed by maestro Stern. Suddenly, he stopped. The audience had not moved, but rather, put on their gasmasks and remained seated in the hall. In an instant, he was back on center stage, raising bow and fiddle, to perform the most exquisite concerto. A gas masked audience sat transfixed, witnessing the performance of a lifetime. Responding to a voice deep within, Isaac Stern played the melody of the Jewish people, "we shall endure." This, too, is the summons to each of us, no matter what the foreboding sirens portend, we are called upon to stand our ground to stay center stage, to play the music of our brief day upon this earth.

How does your dad do all that sad stuff?

To be a rabbi at a congregation of 3,000 families is to see and participate in a multitude of celebrations, baby namings, Bar and Bat Mitzvah, weddings, special birthdays, and anniversaries. To be a rabbi at a congregation of 3,000 families is to witness and share in a lot of sadness, divorce, families torn apart, disease, suicide, and death. Over the course of thirty-six years, dad saw his share of both. Often times, the sad seems to outweigh the happy. From time to time, all professionals come home from a difficult day at work; the conference call was contentious, the deal has been delayed, sales are slower than expected. While these may weigh on us for a period of time, eventually, they seem to subside and we move on. These work issues are not "life and death." But dad's work issues were life and death, holding vigil in the hospital room for a child who is battling leukemia, sitting with a father and young children who have just lost their mom to breast cancer, comforting a family who has lost their beloved father and grandfather. I often wondered how you put those images, that pain, away when your day is over and you come back home.

I also wondered how he "held it together" during all those funerals. I guess because it's his job, he got used to it, but it seems like a daunting task. I remember when my Grandpa Harry died, my dad was the rabbi officiating. This was not some congregant, it was his father-in law, someone who had been a father figure to him. As we stood together a few moments before the service began, I saw a pained look on his face. He then looked down, smiled, and let out a little laugh. Later that afternoon, I asked him about that moment and what he was thinking about. He told me that morning, while getting dressed, he could not decide on a black or dark navy suit. As the funeral service was about to begin, Dad looked down and realized he put on a black suit coat and navy suit pants.

It takes an extraordinary person to deal with all the sadness on a day-to-day basis. Of all of dad's amazing qualities, his ability to minister to people might have been his greatest. Each person in need mattered personally to him. He genuinely cared for each person or each family going through a difficult time. To dad, it was his calling.

There is no greater example of this than the following story.

While at Washington Hospital Center, the day after we learned my father had been diagnosed with a brain tumor, our family was sitting in a hospital examination room as we waited for yet another test. Dad's cell phone rang. It was a family who had just lost a loved one at Washington Hospital Center, the very facility we were at. Dad hung up, jumped off the examination table, buttoned his shirt, fixed his hair, threw on his shoes, and was briskly walking down the hall to be with the family and to comfort them. It did not matter to him that he was in the midst of his own life-changing moment. A congregant was in pain and dad needed to be there for them. That was Joe Weinberg.

Dad was a great minister to people not only because he was incredibly selfless, but he also knew how to be caring and compassionate. Not through prayers, or long words of wisdom, but through simple words, "I am here for you," "I care about you," and simple gestures – a hug, holding someone's hand, cradling a child. Time and time again, I was witness to these simple acts, and each and every time, they made such a difference to those in need. From time to time, dad would publish a commentary in the Temple bulletin, and I still recall one of my favorite entitled *Don't say "I don't know what to say."*

People sometimes struggle with someone else's pain, or experience with death, and have trouble reaching out. Dad's message was the simple acts, the simple words, can do more than you know. It was not something he just wrote about, it was how he dealt with the sadness he encountered each day.

He did all the sad things because he truly believed that was his calling, to be there for others; that was what he was meant to do.

I also think there are two (2) other things that allowed dad to deal with all the sadness he encountered in his rabbinate.

First, he took up jogging. I do not mean he jogged a mile every couple of days. He became a serious runner; six, seven, eight miles every other day. I would constantly hear from my friends, "I saw your dad jogging the other day."

Running, for him, was a chance to clear his mind. To leave the rabbi behind and perhaps the pain, the images, and the challenges. No urgent phone calls, just solitary time were he could be alone in his own thoughts before his day began.

Second, dad made "family time" a top priority. He saw up close how fragile life was, how quickly it all changed, and he was determined to make sure we spent time together. While his schedule was a challenge, he and mom made sure we took advantage of every opportunity for our family to be together whenever possible. If we happened to have a free Saturday or Sunday night, it was dinner and a movie. Although, for this Rabbi and his family, dinner and movie was not, *let's pile into the car head down the street to the local theater and then over to the restaurant around the block.*

While dad loved his congregation, going to dinner down the street was no break from work. It was merely a continuation of office hours, just not at his desk at the Temple. Out at a local restaurant would turn into:

"Rabbi, I hate to bother you but my mother is in the hospital, could you visit her?"

"Rabbi, my son says he wants to drop out of college, what are we to do?"

You get the picture.

To truly have our family time, and allow dad a few hours away from the daily demands, our family night out meant heading to Tysons Corner Virginia. A quick geography lesson. If most of our congregation lived in the Maryland suburbs of Potomac and Bethesda, at the time, there were few congregants who lived across the river in the Virginia suburbs of Washington D.C. At the Tysons Corner Theater, and the local restaurants, we were just a family of five out for a night together.

I vividly recall heading to the restroom at a movie theater with dad one evening at Tysons. I must have been fifteen or sixteen. We each finished our business in the urinal, washed our hands, and as we were drying our hands in front of the large mirror, Dad put his arms around me and said, "You look good, I love you buddy." Not in an emotional way, just like two buddies hanging out.

At that moment, a guy comes out of a stall, shoots us a look and says, "What is you guys? Gay?"

To this day, I always laugh to myself when I visit the restroom at a movie theater.

These nights gave dad the ability to be dad, not rabbi. To enjoy and listen to his kids, to put his arm around them, to laugh and share stories, and, most importantly, to leave the office behind for a few hours.

Time and time again in Dad's sermons, he preached to his congregation to "live life to its fullest," "seize the day," and "celebrate the moment." I saw him countless times stand at the bimah and urge congregants with all of the passion he could muster to "live," not just go through the motions. These were never words on paper. These were words straight from his heart, these were words seared into his soul, for he knew what life could bring in an instant.

WHO OFFICIATED AT YOUR WEDDING?

The same guy who was by my side at my Bar Mitzvah was the rabbi at my wedding. I know what you are thinking. He did the Bar Mitzvah and the wedding, what about the ritual when a Jewish boy is first born, the circumcision? No, Dad never did moonlight as a Moyle (the Jewish term for the person that actually performs the circumcision.) I was told he was just dad for the Jewish ritual.

On June 8, 1991, Mom and Dad walked me down the aisle of Oakwood Country Club in Cleveland, Ohio. Dad gave me a hug and a kiss, and then went around the other side of the Chuppah (the Jewish term for the canopy, or tallit, under which a couple are married under) and put on his robe and tallit over his black tuxedo and performed the wedding ceremony.

Having dad perform my wedding seemed normal to me. For Jennifer, who was about to become a PKIL (preacher's kid in-law,) and did not grow up with a dad as rabbi, it took some getting used to. Most couples go to meet with their rabbi or priest before they get married for pre-marriage counseling. For Jennifer and I, this experience was a little unique.

One Sunday afternoon, about a month before our wedding, we were at brunch at my parent's home. Dad asked Jennifer and I to sit with him in his office for a few minutes. *No big deal*, I thought. He probably wants to go over the logistics for the ceremony, the procession, what prayers we needed to recite, and when do I break the glass. However, as we settled into the couch in his office he started to talk about love and commitment.

"What does it mean to be husband and wife?" has asked.

I could see the look on Jennifer's face; a look of panic that said, "You want me to share these thoughts? Are you the Rabbi or my future father-in-law?"

"Dad," I said. "Shouldn't we talk about the procession? Who walks in with who and when?"

"Relax, Jono," he said. "We will get to all of that, but this is just such an exciting and special time, I just want to hear how you are feeling."

I managed to come up with a few thoughts so we could move the conversation along. I think Jennifer was still trying to figure it all out. We worked through our slightly awkward "counseling session," and made it to the Chuppah.

Right before the ceremony was about to begin, the bridal party lined up, grandparents, groomsmen, bridesmaids, Best Man, Maid of Honor, my parents, and me. The music began, and the procession started. We each waited our turn to walk down the aisle. It was almost my parents turn to begin their walk when Dad turned around, his eyes glistening. He put his hands on my shoulders, and said, "Have a beautiful life."

He turned around, took mom's hand, and began his walk down the aisle. The gesture, those simple words, that moment lives on in my mind. No big speech or sermon, just a father's simple wish for his son's life.

Did your Dad like being a Rabbi?

Rather than having me articulate the answer, I will share with you the sermon my father gave upon his installation as Senior Rabbi at WHC in 1986. I think the sermon provides insight into dad, why he became a rabbi, and what he hoped his rabbinate would mean in the lives of others.

Dad spent his whole life ministering to other people, talking to them, and counseling them about their lives. With Dad, it was always about his congregants and his community, not about him. This sermon is one of the few times he spoke more personally about himself, the person, and his chosen profession.

A rabbi lifts his hands and raises his voice in blessing. For 23 years as a rabbi, I have invoked the beautiful words of our tradition's B'rachat, but tonight, I know, as never before, the meaning of B'racha, of blessing.

"Mah tov Helkeynu, How good is my portion, how pleasant my lot."

I am honored, humbled, challenged and, above all, profoundly moved by this Shabbat and the many cross currents that intersect on this historic evening. To have marked this night of Consecration by receiving the Torah of my Grandpa Opa's synagogue in Germany is overwhelming. Who would ever have thought that the little boy trudging dutifully by his immigrant grandfather through Chicago's Lincoln Park would one day cradle his Torah as rabbi of one of the world's greatest congregations.

And memory tonight will also not let me forget my beloved father-in-law, for whom I was always a son, whose passion and pride was the Jewish people, and who, with my dear mother-in-law, taught me so much about family, love, and sharing. This is a night of thanksgiving as I look out and see my parents, blessed with length of days, graced with 55 years of marriage, and favored by God with the strength to be here as part of the congregation tonight. So much of my own attachment to Judaism and the life of the synagogue has grown out the centrality of Jewish life in my parent's home.

Tonight, I wish most especially to speak to you who are part of my larger family, the members of Washington Hebrew Congregation. You have opened your hearts and your homes to us. Together, we have prayed and studied, danced with the Torah, lifted wine and matzah, but even more importantly, together we have laughed and cried, waited in hospital corridors through anxious moments, tasted the bitter and the sweet. To walk the valleys and the sunlit paths of Chuppah and B'nai Mitzvah to be there for each other, this is what it means to be a congregation.

As a lifetime student, I have been favored to sit in the classroom and lecture hall of brilliant scholars. They ignited an intellectual curiosity, a love and appreciation of our magnificent tradition. Among those whom I treasure are my Uncle Leopold Stern, who was rescued from Dachau to become a Cantor, a religious guide of my family's congregation…

I must say a word about another teacher, without whom this day could never have been possible. Thirty-four years ago, Rabbi Richard Hirsch sent me to the Regional Reform Jewish Summer Camp in Oconomawac, Wisconsin. There, I met Marcia Ellis, and together we began a journey, winding through High School, college, Rabbinic Seminary, three precious children, and a rabbinate of fulfillment, surpassing our most cherished dreams. As partner and teacher, Marcia has taught me many things, but none more valuable than her very special, profound love of people and her intuitive sense of how to reach their souls. In a book review, Marcia spoke of the issue of the role of the Rebbetzen:

"Rebbetzen and rabbi cannot be a role. If it is, you are disingenuous. The rabbinate is not a role, or a profession, or a career. It is a total life, it is who you are."

I have always had a special love of young people, and I am particularly delighted that so many of our children and teenagers are here tonight. But the light of my life when it comes to children is, of course, Rachel, Jonathan, and Joshua. They have educated their aging father, keeping me current with the likes of Madonna, Talking Heads, and The Boss. When they were young, I used to delight in hugging the stuffings out of them, now, two of three are able to return the favor. Those moments of their infancy and childhood were so exquisite in exuberance and so complete with love, I was, for a time, somewhat sad to see them grow. I never imagined what glorious dimensions of sheer joy they would each in the individual and special way bring to my heart as young adults.

Washington Hebrew Congregation is not just another large, prestigious synagogue. We are unique. We are the leading Jewish congregation in the capital of the free world. In this regard, we constantly confront opportunities and solemn responsibilities to be a model of an informed, active religious community, translating the words of Scripture, "Justice, justice shall you pursue," into the itinerary of our daily lives, feeding the hungry, finding shelter for the homeless, bringing hope and compassion to the despairing, the aged and the infirm, bringing economic justice and dignity to the impoverished of our city, reaching out to people of every faith.

The prophetic vision of social justice defines the soul of our religious movement to let the oppressed go free, victims of social injustice in our own land, victims of repression in South Africa, the Soviet Union, El Salvador, and Chile.

I pledge to you tonight my commitment to this work of social justice and moral challenge. I pledge that my colleagues and I will devote our energy and creativity to fashioning for you and your children a Judaism which joyously sings and celebrates our people's ancient faith, a Judaism whose faith will sustain you in dark nights of anguish as well as uplift you in moments of personal simcha.

I pledge a Judaism which is always mindful of the unique and central place of the Land of Israel. We are one people, one faith, ours, in one destiny. Thirty-eight years after the establishment of the State of

Israel, only ten percent of American Jewry have visited Israel. I hope that in the years ahead, every single one of you will take that sacred pilgrimage and know that life changing experience of making the Land of Israel part of our soul.

I pledge to you a rabbinate of integrity, of intellectual and personal honesty. We may not always agree, we may not always be able to say yes, but we will always listen and always care.

I have never forgotten the words which Rabbi Felix Levy spoke to me on my Bar Mitzvah. He talked about the meaning of my name, Yosef, which means, "to add something to". That has always been me, to add to stretch, to reach ever upward, to build ever to create a new. This has always been the very pulse beat of my heart and soul, to ennoble life's meaning and purpose, to make gentle and loving the life of this world.

My biblical namesake, Joseph, served as Pharaoh's governor, second only to the monarch in authority. Yet, when his brothers, who dealt so harshly with him, approached the throne, Joseph could not restrain himself. He reached out in sincere affection and self-disclosure, "Ani Yosef Achicha, I am Joseph, your brother." That shall also be the way of this Joseph, never to withhold, withdraw. Always to reach out to you, Ani Yosef, I am Joseph, here for you.

What was life like after your Dad was diagnosed with his illness?

I once asked my father what he liked best about being a Rabbi. He would say his job allowed him to do so many things wearing one hat. He was a counselor, a writer, an orator, a pastor, a politician, an event planner, an administrator, and a teacher. When pushed as to which of these he enjoyed the most, it was the role of teacher he cherished most.

Over his career, dad must have taught a thousand classes. It was, however, his final lesson, one he taught outside the classroom, that was his greatest teaching moment.

It was late March 1998, and Rabbi Joseph Weinberg, the Senior Rabbi at Washington Hebrew Congregation, was in the middle of a typical busy day. Dad describes it in the Rosh Hashanah sermon he delivered six months later.

> *"In the midst of all of our hectic lives, as we were preparing for the Passover Seder, our congregational trip to Eastern Europe, a family celebration, and interviewing new rabbis, in just one second everything came to a screeching halt with a momentary episode.*
>
> *"It's nothing," I insisted. "I am just hot and tired."*
>
> *But we checked it out at the hospital anyway. And then the word came back – Brain Tumor. This can't be. I do not have time for this. I am too busy. But the reality would not go away. Suddenly, a wonderful healthy life, planning and thinking of forever, turned into, would there be another day? Would there be a tomorrow?*
>
> *Two days later, at the hospital, I kissed Marcia and the children. We prayed, and then the gurney was wheeled into the operating room. Hours later, as I opened my eyes and came back to life, I whispered the prayer, "Blessed are you ,Oh God, who lifts up the fallen and brings*

your creation back to life" Within days I was walking the streets of New York."

Several days following surgery, we got the news the doctors had predicted when they discovered the tumor; malignant.

I am certain that, as a Rabbi for over thirty years, who had ministered to hundreds in times of illness, and who knew every square inch of every hospital in the Washington, D.C. area, dad was aware of what a malignant tumor meant. If he was scared or angry or filled with sadness, he never showed it. He would, on occasion, lament this whole thing was not fair to the family. He did not dwell on his illness or the long days of treatment ahead. Instead, he began to teach.

After surgery, dad began round after round of radiation and chemotherapy, but he never slowed down. He continued to perform weddings, conduct services, and care for his congregants. He led a trip to Israel where he even went parasailing over the Red Sea. To be sure, there were doctor visits, tests, conversations about treatments, but those discussions didn't last long. Dad would not allow it. His focus was on that day, the appointment with a potential donor, a meeting with a couple he was going to marry, babysitting that night for a grandchild, or finding the right house at the beach for our family vacation that summer.

In September, it was Rosh Hashanah eve. As we sat in the sanctuary prior to the start of services, I, like the rest of the family, was trying to "hold it together." So much was swirling in our heads, but chief among was the question, "Would this be dad's final high holidays?" The music began, and the rabbis and cantor began the procession from the rear of the sanctuary. While everyone turned around to see the clergy, I remember telling myself, *Look ahead. Be strong.*

But in mid-procession, something inside of me said, *Turn around. Do not miss this moment, bear witness to this triumph.*

The operating room at New York University Hospital seemed like a distant memory. Dad looked wonderful in his brilliant white robe and multi-colored tallit. His eyes were beaming and his face shown with a look of pride and determination.

His sermon that night, not surprisingly, dealt with how precious our lives are. He said:

> *"As we get older, we can't wait for the school year to end. At work, we wait for vacation to begin. Don't wish the days away. Each one is too dear. When I walked out of the hospital last April, the outdoors almost took my breath away, the sky was so blue, the grass so green, the buds on the trees ready to burst, the laughter of the children so crisp and clear. Seize the day, dear friends! God forbid that it should ever take illness to see the majesty of every new dawn."*

Dad preached a beautiful sermon, recited the Avinu Malkeinu (a sacred prayer read during the High Holiday days) as strong as ever, blessed his congregation, and when the service was complete, sat in his office with a glass of water and a slew of anti-nausea pills before conducing the late service that night.

For the next seven months, life was normal, or as our family termed it, our "new normal."

Every six to eight weeks, Dad had to have an MRI to check to see if his tumor had come back. To get the results of the MRI, we had to go to Duke Medical Center, where dad's oncologists were based. While we dreaded the moment in the doctor's office when they delivered the results of the MRI, the journey down to Interstate 85 to Durham, North Carolina become the center of wonderful family times.

Dad described in a sermon:

> *"Marcia and I were making plans for our routine trip to Duke to see my doctor. First one, then another, and finally all three of our children decided they wanted to come along, and so, the five of us found ourselves in the car for a four and a half hour ride to Durham. What a time we had, talking, laughing, and remembering."*

To say we looked forward to those trips would be lying. We dreaded them. But on the other hand, there were so many moments of pure joy, of family togetherness as we winded south down the interstate. I remember one night in a hotel room where a small laugh at something on the television turned into giggles. The giggles turned into laughter, which then turned into uncontrollable laughter, with all of us doubled over in pain. We would sit at a Cracker Barrel somewhere near Richmond and be amazed that dad, the one with the brain tumor, was still the only one who solve the "Peg Game" found at the table. We would take walks around Duke Gardens, gazing at the Carolina blue sky and the deep red of the crepe myrtles. We would sit in the car and discuss current events or a sermon idea or recount the latest grandchild story.

We knew what lay at the end of these trips. A defining moment with our doctor and news that would literally mean life or death. But as dad taught us during these months, and during the trips, life was not about the destination, it was about the journey; living each moment, each day, to its fullest.

WHAT WAS THE MOST MEMORABLE SERVICE YOUR DAD EVER OFFICIATED AT?

In May of 1999 it had been just over twelve months since Dad's brain tumor was discovered. He had endured round after round of chemotherapy and radiation treatments. Early in that month brought the news I think we all knew we would hear one day, but wished it wasn't for another 12 years. Dad's tumor was back. Dad and our family were not ready to give up. Over brunch at my parent's home, we all decided we would continue to fight.

The next week, our family traveled to Durham, North Carolina for surgery number two. The procedure was set for Monday morning. The day before was Mother's Day. This year, Mother's Day would not be celebrated with a big brunch at my parent's home, but rather at Duke Hospital, and preparing Dad for his second brain surgery. We still, however, went out to dinner that night. Dad insisted we take mom out and celebrate her day. He would not have it any other way.

The next day, Dad came through the five-hour surgery well. In two days, he was up and walking. Two days after brain surgery, Joe Weinberg was walking the halls of Duke Hospital. Dad was always an impatient patient. He wanted out quickly. They asked him to walk down the hospital corridor one time, and dad went up and back four times. When they told him to do his breathing exercises five or six times, he would do ten. He seemed to be in a hurry these days, like had somewhere to be. Indeed he did.

Six days after surgery to remove a portion of his tumor from his brain, dad, his head wrapped in white bandages, stood in front the Washington Hebrew Confirmation Class of 1999, a class that would be his last. He addressed the class in a simple, beautiful, and courageous manner. This is what he had to say:

> *What a wonderful class you are. I can't remember a sweeter, kinder group of young men and women, and I would not have missed to day for anything; and there were a few bumps in the road to get here!*

You have chosen as your Confirmation theme "The Time of Your Life." The founder of Chasidim, the Bal Shem Tov, had the same idea when he wrote: "The world is new every morning, that is God's gift and a person should believe he is reborn each day." What a wonderful thought, each day a fresh gift given to each one of us. How, then, shall you, as committed young Jews, use this special gift?

First of all, Judaism tells us not to worry about being happy. Happiness will flow from the involvements you form, "Do not ask if life was good to you, but rather were you good to life." Judaism says, "Make a difference" in the world, be God's partner in repairing our tattered earth. "Justice, justice shall you pursue" demands the prophet, and so many of you answered that call with your service projects and your understanding of mitzvot.

Judaism is also a religion of memory, of remembering those who have come before us. Many of you spoke so movingly today about your grandparents and parents, and how much they mean to you. Understand that you also need to live your life as a role model for the next generation. You will be the moms and dads who shape the world for those who come after you.

Life is moving very fast for you, dear friends. Yesterday, it seemed, was Bar and Bat Mitzvah, today Confirmation, tomorrow graduation. Do not let time go by aimlessly. Seize the day! Live each day to the fullest, this is always the time of your life.

May all God's choicest blessings be yours. Please know that Washington Hebrew Congregation is always here for you. Now that you can drive, don't forget to come see us. This is always your home.

Zeh Ha Yom Asa Adoni, "This is the day God has made, let us rejoice and be glad therein"

Amen.

If you are ever in Washington D.C. and visit Washington Hebrew Congregation, you will notice the hallway lined with Confirmation Class pictures through the years. Look for the 1999 class picture. There you will find Dad, front and center, robe, tallit, head wrapped in bandages, smiling, and so very proud.

What was your Dad's last sermon?

In the late summer of 1999, the MRI did not look good, and we learned that Dad's tumor had come back yet again. As Rosh Hashanah approached, it was becoming apparent Dad would have a difficult time delivering a High Holiday sermon. However, our father was not going to give in.

"I have a lot to say to my congregation," he would say.

Dad went to work on his sermon, a sermon he termed his ethical will, a bequest of a spiritual legacy for those who would follow. It would be a summation of what he learned in life and what he wished for his loved ones. On Rosh Hashanah eve, my sister, brother, and I stood with our father and took turns reading his words. Dad read the beginning of the sermon and the last paragraph. He spoke with more passion, more conviction, than we have ever heard before. The following was the last sermon of Rabbi Joseph Weinberg entitled, *Still Alive.*

> *Thirty-two Rosh Hashanahs ago, I first stood before you in this sanctuary. The wood paneling was dark, there were no windows, and the seats were blue-green. Vietnam was swirling all around us, the Democratic convention in Chicago had just nominated Hubert Humphrey as their candidate while young people rioted outside and delegates screamed at each other inside. Richard Nixon would soon be elected President and Watergate would follow.*
>
> *But in 1968, I stood here in this sanctuary, thirty-one years old, overwhelmed with the honor of being able to serve such an outstanding congregation. You were, at that moment, just a sea of faces, but at each succeeding New Year, more and more of you were known to me. This one I married, and that one's baby I named, this one's father I buried, I danced at this one's wedding, and sat with this family at a hospital*

bedside. We have shared so much together; the good, the bad, the laughter, and the tears.

You are now so much my family, giving me your prayers and concern, that I could not think of missing this night. And so, two weeks ago, when again we heard that I must battle anew with my pesky invader, I vowed to have Rosh Hashanah as usual. I am, as you know, a determined rabbi. Some former congregational presidents might say "stubborn," but I like "determined" better. However, I made one concession to my family. I would accept their help in delivering my remarks. Since the beginning of this challenge, they have surrounded me with their special love and support, and so it is very fitting that they physically stand with me now. The words are mine, but for the remainder of my sermon, I will speak through the voices of Rachel, Jonathan, and Joshua.

Ma Nish Ta Na Halila HaZeh, "Why is this night different from all others?"

No, I do not have the wrong holiday, I am asking why is this Rosh Hashanah different from all others? The answer is that this is the last Rosh Hashanah of the 20th century, and of this millennium. It makes a time already set aside for meditation and contemplation even more awesome.

What will fill the days and years of the 21st century? We peer into the fog that hangs over the next century, but we cannot pierce the haze that is the future. Winston Churchill tried to predict things for a while, and then gave up, complaining that, "the future was just one damned thing after another!" People speak of the "foreseeable future," but that is an oxymoron.

So, we will not attempt the impossible. Instead, tonight, I would like to spend a little time asking another question:

"What advice do the inhabitants of the 20th century wish to give to those who will lead in 21st century?"

Giving such advice, and I would suggest that every one of you do the same as you sit around your festival table tomorrow, is a very time-

honored tradition. It is called an ethical will. Its aim is to bequeath a spiritual legacy to those who will follow us. When we think of a will, we usually envision a legal document intended to divide up one's material possessions. But ethical wills are left behind in the belief that the wisdom and insights acquired in a lifetime are as much a part of a family's legacy as all the "stuff" we acquire.

The patriarch, Jacob, gathered his children around and tried to tell them the way in which they should live. Since that time, Jews have tried to sum up what they have learned in life and what they want for their loved ones.

And so, on this birthday of the world, I write my statement to those who I pray will live deep into the 21st century, my grandchildren:

Dear Zachary, Haley, Dani, and Jake (and I know, Dad) those that yet shall be (At the time of the sermon, my brother, Josh, did not have any kids yet.)

You are all asleep in your beds, all snug and warm with so many stuffed animals that I can hardly find your faces. There is no better picture than this. But I have seen other images this day, frightened little children, just your age, holding hands, being led away from the horror at the North Valley Jewish Community Center in Los Angeles, another in a long line of shootings, Littleton, Jonesboro, Atlanta, Skokie. How often have we seen teenagers racing for their lives out of a terror-filled school, children sobbing uncontrollably at a playmate's funeral, or parents walking their children to the bus stop, afraid to even let go of their child's precious hand. Offices, schools, rural areas, urban centers, no place is safe anymore.

There are very few things we can tell the inhabitants of the next century that is more important than this: the gun madness must end!

Each year, almost 33,000 people die from gunshot wounds, and of them, 8,800 are under the age of twenty-four. The New England Journal of Medicine reported that it "is 43 times more likely for a handgun kept in the home to be used against its owner, a family member, or friend, than to be used successfully against an intruder,"

It was late at night last summer when a mother began telling me her story.

"We had a child before our other two children were born," she said. "He was twenty-two months old and I brought him to the babysitter's house. The sitter had a four year old child and the sitter's husband had a gun in the house. Somehow, the gun was found by the 4 year old, shots were fired, and our 22-month-old son lay dead."

It took just an instant to happen sixteen years ago, but the reverberations are forever. The guns must go! Let there be hunting clubs for those who wish to hunt. There the guns can be safely stored, but let us get this plague out of homes and off our streets.

This is a huge undertaking, my dear grandchildren and inhabitants of the 21st century, for I am asking you to tackle a gigantic problem and, in some circles, still a very unpopular cause. I speak of the gun issue now because clearly the safety of our children is at risk. Easily one can cry out on this subject, on any subject, "I am only one person. What can I do?"

I am sure you will be asked more than once in your lifetime to step forward and take a stand. Remember, always, that Judaism tells us that every person is a partner with God and every person can make a difference.

The poet Aaron Zeitlin wrote:

> *Praise me says Go, I will know that you love me.*
> *Cure me, I will know that you love me.*
> *Praise me or curse me*
> *I will know that you love me.*
> *But if you sit fenced off in your apathy*
> *Entrenched in "I don't care" says God*
> *If you see suffering and do not cry out*
> *If you don't praise and don't revile*
> *The I created you in vain says God*

Failure is not the problem, only one's unwillingness to try. Even if you don't have faith in yourself, God has faith in you. Judaism's great mis-

sion for us in life is "tikkun olam," the repairing of the world. "It is not the critic who counts," Theodore Roosevelt once said. "The credit belongs to the man who is actually in the arena; who strives valiantly; who knows the great enthusiasms, the great devotions and spending himself in a worthy cause."

Get involved! Care about issues, your community, your people. And know that you are never alone. For one person joins another and another, and the world can change.

A true story is told of a Friday evening service at a synagogue in Lyon France, at the beginning of the Nazi occupation. As is the custom during the singing of La Cha Do De, the worshippers stand and, when they sing the words to welcome the Sabbath bride, the congregation turns to the front of the doors as a greeting. Unknown to the worshippers, the Nazis had decided to begin deporting the Jews that very night. The soldiers ran up the stairs of the synagogue and pulled open the front doors just as the entire congregation turned to greet the Sabbath bride. So shocked were the Nazis by what they saw as this show of solidarity, that they actually turned around and left the sanctuary.

It is not often that you feel the strength of community so dramatically, but several times in my life, I have had the privilege of connecting with others in such a powerful way.

It was 1965 in Alabama. Martin Luther King Jr. had called for the faith community to join him in a freedom march from Selma to Montgomery and I, with other rabbis, answered that call. Side by side, black and white, Jew and gentile, we clasped hands and walked together. All around people were yelling, taunting, even spitting at us. Alone, we would never have had a chance, but together, we faced down hatred and fear and turned a small corner in the America's civil rights struggle.

Many years later, in a forest outside Moscow, members of Washington Hebrew Congregation sat with the refusenik community, Jews who had been denied visas to immigrate. We picnicked, studied Torah, sang Israeli songs, and danced the Hora. All the while, the KGB stood at the edge of the clearing with their billy clubs in hand, "Am Yisrael

Chai" we sang. The Russian Jews refused to be intimidated and, slowly, with the wonderful work of so many of you on behalf of Soviet Jewry, cracks began to appear in the Iron Curtain. "Let our People Go" we chanted, we marched until the curtain came crashing down. In such moments, you know that people united in purpose and action can truly move mountains.

I know that it is not easy to have faith in people today. There is too much hypocrisy and hatred. The world is a cynical place. We in the 20th century have witnessed such cruelty, acted so barbarically, that the human suol has been all but crushed. The Holocaust was indeed our darkest hour, but even right up to the last minute of this century, man continue to act more like beast than human.

Internationally, Sierra Leone, Angola, and Kosovo, rounding up whole families, locking them in their homes, and then setting their house ablaze. Right here, in our own community, two teenage boys plot to murder, then kill, dismember, and burn another human being. Our stomachs turn in revulsion. The murder, maiming, rape, and pillage make us tremble in fear for the next generation.

We wonder how can we regain our faith.

I remember a night this summer, as I sat on the beach with the family and looked up at the sky. Sometimes, the night was covered with clouds that it looked pitch black. And at other times, the heavens twinkled with a million stars. In the same way, just when one feels all hope is lost, the spark of the Devine placed in each of us can burst forth to light the world.

After the terrible Turkish earthquake last month, we saw doctors and nurses from Greece, arch enemies of the Turks, coming immediately to the aid of their neighbors. "I will never again speak ill of the Greeks," said one grateful patient. "They saved my life."

And witness the incredible buoyancy of the human spirit as manifest in the unbelievable story of cyclist Lance Armstrong. Three years ago, Armstrong lay in a hospital bed with testicular cancer which had already spread to his lungs and brain. Attacking cancer like the fierce competitor he is, Armstrong refused to give up. After extensive therapy, he put himself through the most taxing training program imaginable. Three years later, Armstrong was on his bicycle in a grueling 21 day, 2,300 mils test of endurance. On July 25th, in Paris, he was first to cross the finish line, making him the Tour de France champion. (In 1999, Dad, like all of us, was in awe of what Lance Armstrong was able to accomplish. Today, we know the truth.)

But my own favorite story of the human spirit goes to Christopher Cassidy, the 9-year-old son of our Director of Finance here at WHC. Born with muscular dystrophy and destined to end up in a wheel chair if a cure is not found, Christopher shrugs this off with, "everybody has something." Christopher decided early on that he did not want to be "special;" he wanted to be like all the other boys and girls and that meant joining the swim team. Given his degenerative disease, he has a 1 in a 1,000 shot of every winning a race, but into the water he goes, time and time again, always coming in sixth, last place. And then, several weeks ago, with spectators cheering wildly, he tied for 5th.

"I can do this, I am getting better," he enthusiastically shouted. "I am a winner."

"The soul is God's candle," the Book of Proverbs tells us. What a mighty flame this little boy has kindled.

We have spoken tonight about getting involved in the issues of the day, daring to make a difference in the world, and having faith in the power of the human spirit. And let me add just one more, use time wisely. Many of us subscribe to Time Magazine and, once a year, we receive a renewal notice with a card that reads, "Send me another 52 weeks of Time."

That is exactly what we ask on this Rosh Hashanah. Give us more time, O God. There is so much yet to do. There is a story of any angry reader who stormed into a newspaper office waving the day's paper, asking to see the editor of the obituary column. He showed him his name in the obituary listing.

"You see," he said, "I am very much alive. I demand a retraction!" The reporter replied, "I never retract a story. But I tell you what I will do. I'll put you in the birth announcements and give you a fresh start." Rosh Hashanah is God's great gift to us, a fresh start. The precious gift of time, the hours of our days, the days of our years, the years of our life. They are all ours, ours to fill wisely, joyfully, completely.

The privilege of being alive was beautifully expressed by the great Russian author, Leo Tolstoy. During the last years of his life, he began each day's journal entry in his diary with the words, "Still alive, The breath of life is still within me." Dear congregants, children, and grandchildren: It is Rosh Hashanah 5760, and we are still here, Still alive, to stand for causes that are just, Still alive to stand in solidarity with others, still alive to bear witness to the majesty of the human soul. Still Alive! Still Alive! God bless you, now, and always.

Amen.

A little less than a month after standing on the bimah with his children and delivering his final sermon to his congregation, on a Friday night, with the Shabbat candles slowing burning down, mom, Rachel, Josh, and I surrounded our dad and held his hand as he passed away.

Do you still miss your Dad; does it get easier as time goes by?

I was paying a condolence call to a friend that had recently lost his dad. Surrounded by a group of people, I heard a woman trying to comfort my friend. "Don't worry, it will get easier as time goes by."

A few minutes later, my friend looked at me, "Really?"

Not really. While the shock of losing a parent eventually subsides, and your life without your parent becomes the "new normal," the loss and the pain that comes with it never really goes away. There is rarely a day that goes by since his passing that I do not think about my dad. Not every memory leads me to sadness; there are plenty of laughs and smiles that the memory of my dad brings to my face. There are so many places and occasions were the memory of my father still burns bright.

At every high holiday service since my father's death, I can close my eyes and I still see him. As the cantor and choir chant, "We are your people," he is there, in his familiar spot, first chair to the left of the Ark. His multi-color tallit against his bright white robe. His folder filled with papers tucked inside his prayer book. The slight adjustment to his glasses, his hand pushing his part over through his salt and pepper hair. His gaze out to the congregation, often times looking for where mom, Rachel, Josh, and I were sitting to give us a smile. And then the cantor and choir come to the closing of their song, rising from his seat, striding toward the bimah, a purpose, a determination in his face.

On the one (1) year anniversary of Dad's passing, as our family prepared for the service in which we would dedicate the tombstone at his gravesite, I wrote the following about missing my dad:

Dear Dad:

Last Saturday morning, I went out to buy a grill. In no time I was at the store, had the right model picked out, loaded into my car, and was back at the house. I unpacked all of the pieces and lay them across the garage floor, and I waited. I was waiting for you to show up so we could begin to work.

"He must have gotten caught up at Temple," I thought as I looked at my watch.

Then, I caught myself, reality set in, you were not coming to help me. Tears began to well up and I sat there on my garage floor and began to cry.

Dad, I started to try to put the pieces together but nothing fit. I needed you there. Why was this so hard? Why so emotional to put a grill together? Certainly there have been so many moments that I have felt the pain of not having you with us. Every birthday party, seeing Zack and Haley holding hands as they jumped into the pool together, sitting in the hospital waiting room waiting for Josie to be born, or setting the Passover table, why now, why was this so difficult?

I realized that during so much of the year I missed you for others. For Zachary and Danielle not having their Papa Joe to play with, for Mom and Rachel and Josh not having you with them, but sitting on the floor of my garage, Dad, I missed you for me.

How many times did you and I work together to assemble a grill, a toy, or a bicycle. We would huddle over the directions, usually not written in English, trying to figure out which piece went where, all the while catching up, talk of family, or how work was going, current events, a funny story, or a sermon idea; it was the two of us, it was our time.

Seventy-three pieces dad, seventy-three pieces. The salesman at the store said it would be easy to put together. I dried the tears and began to laugh to myself thinking of how often we would struggle with an "easy assembly job."

I began to pick up the pieces and go to work. As the pieces stared to fall into place, I found myself catching up with you, just as we used to do, recounting a funny story of something one of the kids had recently done, updating you on my community involvements, thinking about a difficult issue at work, I went through it all with you.

Several hours later, I was done. The grill was complete. I sat for a moment staring at the finished product and shed another tear or two. Dad, I realize while it is not like it used to be, and it hurts, you are still by my side. You have not really left me, or any of us. You are there, ready to build and assemble, ready to talk, to listen, to cry or to laugh; always by my side.

I wrote the following on the tenth anniversary of his passing:

Back to Churchill

On a crisp, Fall Friday night in October 1999, I attended a Churchill High School football game. There was nothing extraordinary about going to a Churchill game on a Friday night. As a graduate of the school, and living in the area, I have been to my share of games. However, this night was different. This night was special. With me was my father, mother, and my four-year old son. It was 18 months previous to that night my father had been diagnosed with a brain tumor. Through two surgeries, numerous chemotherapy treatments, and radiation cycles, it was becoming more apparent to our family we were losing Dad. That night, the Churchill football team paid tribute to Dad, by wearing white ribbons on their uniforms, a sign that they were thinking of him. As I tried to keep track of my son, who kept running up and down the bleachers, people kept coming up to our family to give Dad a hug and say hello. In the midst of the cold reality time was slipping away, the night was filled with warmth, with embraces, and with another reality of just how many people cared and loved Dad. One week later, late on Friday night, Dad passed away.

Ten years later, on a cool evening in October, I am back in the stands at Churchill High School. The benches, the field, the setting, all the same, only the sport being played is different. Tonight it is soccer, not football, and the four-year old is not with me climbing up and down the stands. He is now fourteen and is on the field as a freshman soccer player. As I watch my son run up and down the field, my mind turns to Dad, with so many emotions running through my brain.

"How I wish he were here to see him."

"How can it be ten years already?"

Ten years is now one quarter of my entire life not to have had my father. As much as I try to convince myself that, in some ways, Dad is still with me, and I know he would have been proud of me and my family, I would still like to hear it from him. I would still like to see him see my kids with his own eyes. The sadness catches up with me. But before I can let it overtake me, I see my son make a great play on the field, working as hard as he possibly can. Slowly, the sadness is pushed back, the joy and the pride of the moment take hold.

As evening gave way to night, it was midway through the second half when my son scored what turned out to be the winning goal. Dad would have loved it. But since he can't be here to see it, I will enjoy it twice as much, once for me and once for him.

CONCLUSION

ARE YOU GOING TO BE A RABBI WHEN YOU GROW-UP?

2A. Now that is more like it.

It is some six (6) months after the night I found myself staring at that stack of sermons on my desk. The deal has closed. What I suspected about my future at the company has come to fruition, in a few months, they will be laying me off.

If the business traveler knows right away about 31E, he or she will also quickly recognize what 2A is all about. First Class. I am on my way to Jackson Hole, Wyoming for a trip my company has planned to thank those who helped complete the deal. As I settle into my roomy and comfortable leather seat, the reality that, in a few months, I will be out of work begins to take hold and, as it does, the second most popular question a PK can get floats to the forefront of my brain, "Are you going to be a rabbi when you grow-up?"

This was a question asked mostly when I was younger by the elderly ladies stuffing brownies into their pocket books during an Oneg Shabbat. It was asked, on occasion, by the parents of my friends when I was back home on break from college. A logical question. There are many families with long traditions of sons following in their father's footsteps and becoming rabbis.

Me, a rabbi?

It did cross my mind from time to time. To be sure, I admired my dad. I felt proud when I was sitting in the congregation as he thundered away an important message from the bimah; felt proud and lucky to have him as my dad when a congregant would tell me how much they admired him, or how he had made an important difference in their lives. At the same time, when I was younger, I would be getting ready for a football Sunday in front of the T.V. when I would see dad dashing out of the house in the dark suit for a day that included back to back funerals. I thought to myself, *Poor guy, does he know the games he is going to miss today?*

At the time, I thought the job caused him to miss out. I think, at times, maybe dad thought that as well. I do not think he regretted his decision to become a Rabbi. If I could ask him if he had it to do all over again, would he be a rabbi, I have not a doubt in the world his answer would be a resounding "yes." However, his profession had its trade-offs. I guess most professions do. Maybe just not as pronounced as the life of a Rabbi.

A few times, when I was with dad and a congregant would shoot me the question, "Are you going to be a rabbi like your dad when you grow-up?" Dad would sometimes jokingly steer the question away.

"A Rabbi? No, he is going to be sportscaster. You should hear him in front of the television with the sound down as he broadcasts the play-by play of the game. He is going to be the next Howard Cosell," he would tell them.

In a way, I think that was dad's hidden message to me, while the life a rabbi is incredibly rewarding, it is also incredibly demanding. I never had any real discussions with him about entering the rabbinate. Law school was the direction I went after college. I look back on my relationship with my father with almost no regrets, and with nothing but a full heart of the most wonderful memories. But now, with my professional career in transition, I think maybe I should have hit the pause button out of college. Maybe I should have had that discussion with him. Me? A Rabbi?

While I did not follow my father's formal path and become a rabbi. I think (and I hope) that I have emulated and followed much of what he believed and much of what he stood for. I think back to the wonderful family trips and cruises I have taken my family on; memories which last a lifetime, and I know that love of family and importance of taking time to be together came from dad. I am happy with the number of non-profit organizations and causes I have associated myself with over the years, and I know getting involved, standing up for what I believe in, this, too, came from my father. I have become a runner, not to the extent of my dad, but I run my fair share. Out on the roads in the early morning, I understand the quiet and solitude my Dad must have enjoyed. I have taken to cooking. I love to create a wonderful meal for the family.

My favorite is to recreate Dad's matzah crunch at Passover, or his world famous Baked Alaska for a birthday celebration. And yes, I even keep the dishtowel over the shoulder in true Joe Weinberg style. I know all of these things did not just come out of thin air, but it was because of what I saw growing up – it came from dad.

I did not follow Dad's occupational profession, but I hope, in many ways, I have followed his path – his path of family, of values and ideas, and of serving others.

I still, to this day, constantly run into people at a restaurant, on the soccer fields during my kids' games, and certainly in the Krieger Lobby at Washington Hebrew Congregation, and hear the similar refrain:

"I miss your dad."

"He meant so much to my family."

"I will never forget the story..."

Those same people often say, "I am sure you get tired of hearing this."

To the absolute contrary, it never gets old, it never gets tiring. It does remind me to try to be more like him. I'm not leaving my legal career for the Rabbinate (although, I do have a lot of sermon topics). Those interactions push me to listen to his words, act on the messages he dedicated his life to. In doing that, I think I can say I followed in his footsteps.

"Excuse me sir, would you like a hot towel?" Ah, the life in First Class. The days are ticking away; my next chapter awaits. I do not face it with an overwhelming sense of sadness or pessimism. Quite the opposite, I am curious and excited to see what lies ahead.

A few days before my trip out west, I ran into a family friend at the grocery store. After some small talk she says, "I see that your company was acquired, do you know what that means for you?"

"I am not sure," I replied.

"Have you ever considered becoming a rabbi like your dad?"

A FINAL NOTE

Writing this book and answering all of the PK questions has given me the wonderful opportunity to reflect back on so many memories of my father, something one does not get to do often in the hectic pace of our lives. Writing this book has been a gift. The gift of memory. It once again breathes life into my dad, even after he has been gone so many years. Dad once spoke about this gift, and what it can mean in a Yiskor sermon in 1997. He said:

> *"This is a time of missing, of longing, of reaching out to embrace those who are not here. And yet, as the shadows of the day begin to lengthen, we become increasingly introspective. We discover the most amazing miracle, suddenly, our loved ones are by our side. They have come to visit us. We can, if we allow ourselves, to almost feel the touch of their hands, the warmth of their embrace. And surely, if we permit ourselves and close our eyes, we will see them once more, not frail or weakened by years or illness, not the last chapter of their lives, but those strong, beautiful images, moments of celebration, a bar or bat mitzvah ceremony, standing under the Chuppah, a birthday party, running on the beach, gathered around the Thanksgiving or Passover table.*
>
> *Death may have ended the life of a loved one, but the relationship does not cease. Relationship continues."*

And so it has.